T0077870

CHARLES PHILLIPS

What is the GOSPEL *that* JESUS CHRIST *taught while on this* EARTH?

authorHOUSE®

AuthorHouse™
1663 Liberty Drive
Bloomington, IN 47403
www.authorhouse.com
Phone: 833-262-8899

Scripture taken from the Holy Bible, King James Version (Authorized Version). First published in 1611. Quoted from the KJV Classic Reference Bible, Copyright © 1983 by The Zondervan Corporation.

Published by AuthorHouse 09/10/2020

ISBN: 978-1-7283-7151-1 (sc)
ISBN: 978-1-7283-7382-9 (e)

Print information available on the last page.

This book is printed on acid-free paper.

CONTENTS

INTRODUCTION

The Holy Scriptures is the oldest history record we have today. Begins with the Creation of this world and the creation of mankind and how God created the heavens and the earth, the light, the water, and dry land. Then God created man in His own image, and put him in dominion over all He had created. Tells how all this was done in six days and said it was good. Then we read that God rested the seventh day from all His work.

In this age today, there are many ministers who preach a Gospel, and communion with God will impart to the minister's a power greater than the influence of his preaching. The heart of the 'true' minister is filled with the intense longing to save souls.

In apostolic times, Satan has led the Jews to exalt the ceremonial law and reject Christ; today Satan induces many Christians under the pretense of honoring Christ, and casting contempt on the moral Law and teach that its precepts may be transgressed with impunity.

If ministers of the Gospel were to bear constantly in mind, the fact that they are dealing with the purchased blood of Christ, they would have a deeper sense of the importance of their work. Some leaders and ministers are determined that the work of preaching the Gospel must be conducted in accordance with their own ideas. These preachers have lost sight of the fact that God is the teacher of His people. Let no one feel he is stepping down in becoming a child of God. Christ hung upon Calvary's Cross, dying in our behalf, that we might have eternal life. Is it a small thing that

He should endure all this that we might be called the sons and daughters of God ?

It is hard for some to accept the Truth of the Gospel when all their life they have honored for Truth is only the idea's of the one that was put out of Heaven because he wanted to worship God as he pleased. The Gospel has always achieved its greatest success among the humbler classes of Christians. Among professing ministers there are always some who preach their opinions instead of the Word of God. The growing contempt for the Law of God is making a distaste for religion, and a increase of pride, love for pleasure, disobedience to parents and authority.

The great truth's necessary for salvation are made clear as noonday in the Holy Scripture's. No one will make a mistake or lose their way, except those who follow their own judgment instead of the plainly revealed truth in the Gospel of God.

THE GOSPEL OF LOVE!

The first time "Gospel" is used in Scripture is found in 'Matt 4:23'—"and Jesus went about all Galilee, teaching in the synagogues, and preaching the Gospel of the kingdom, and healing all manner of sickness and all manner of disease among the people. God's Holy Word has been handed down to us today, at such a cost of suffering and blood by the Waldenses, John Wycliffe, Huss and Jerome, Martin Luther and others that helped and protected them. Never forget ! Some think it is proof of superior talent and learning to explain away God's most important Truth's, and rejecting its Author.

The Gospel is a strong affection for or attachment or devotion to a person or persons. Love is the benevolent love of God for mankind, and that people should have for each other.

Your eternal life depends on the Love and the Word of God, not what we hear from some people who should know, but from God's Word 'Holy Bible' for His word has never changed—Mal 3:6 ; Isa 31:2—Ps 89:34—1 Sam 15:29—Num 23:19. The Word of God will never change. Make the Bible your foundation of your hope and faith, and not the traditions of men or what is popular with the world.

Was the Gospel different for the people before the Flood, than those after the flood? What about Abraham and the children of Israel? Do we have a new Gospel today to live by? The Gospel has and will be forever the same for every person on earth since creation and is the same for all the host of heaven. The Gospel is simple enough for all to understand, and is found in the commandments of God. All the heavens in the universe honor the Law of God and His Law is not hard to understand. God's law is about God's love for His creation of mankind and our love for our fellowmen, and our love for our Creator. There is no force in the Law of God. Love has no force involved in it.

The Gospel is the message that brings joy, hope, and salvation from sin. The Gospel is a message for all people. How do we know this is true? [John 3:16] "For God so loved the world, that He gave His only begotten Son, that whosoever "believeth" in Him should not perish, but have everlasting life."

This assurance we have that the poor have equal rights to the Gospel with the rich, is the fact that the first announcement of the birth of Christ was to men of humble life. It was not to the chief priest and Scribes nor nobles. The Gospel is not beyond the understanding of uneducated people.

The one thing the world is seeking after is power. Some seek it by means of wealth or politics, others by education. Consequently, none of these things satisfy a person. He who planted a desire in man, is the only one who can satisfy it. [Haggai 2:7] "the desire of all nations, shall come; and I will fill this house with glory, saith the Lord of Hosts.

There is a strange and solemn power in the words of Scripture that speak directly to the hearts of those who are longing for Truth. It is the voice of God, and to carry conviction to those who hear and study the Gospel of Truth. Christians today are to be the salt of the earth. Matt 5:13—"Ye are the salt of the earth." How can that be? We should make others thirsty for the Gospel of Truth !

Power is what men desire, and the Lord wants man to have power, but the power which men seek would ruin them. The power which the Lord desires for man to have, is power that will save them. The Gospel brings to all men power. Creation shows the creative power of God, and since the Gospel is the power of God unto salvation, it follows that the Gospel is the power to save mankind from sin.

So what does the Gospel consist of? The Gospel is the good news of salvation through Christ and Him crucified, for the Gospel is the power of God unto salvation. The doctrine of the second advent is the very keynote of the Scriptures. "—1 Thessalonians 4:16—"Behold, He cometh with clouds; and every eye shall see Him."—Rev 1:7 The Lord Himself shall decent from heaven with a shout, with the voice of the Archangel, and with the trump of God,

Matt 4:23—"Jesus went about all Galilee teaching in their synagogues, and preaching the Gospel of the Kingdom" —. Mark 1:14-15—"Jesus came to Galilee preaching the Gospel of the kingdom of God."

The Gospel is the record of this world and all that was made, and by Whom and how it was made. We can read this in John 1: 1-14. "In the beginning was the Word, and the Word was with God, and the Word was God. All things were made by Him; and without Him was not any thing made that was made. In Him was life; and the life was the light of men.—He was in the world, and the world was made by Him, and the world knew Him not. He came unto His own, and His own received Him not. But as many as received Him, to them He gave power to become the sons of God. He was the only begotten of the Father, full of grace and truth." [Colossians 1:17] "He is before all things, and by Him all things consist."

The everlasting Gospel is the preaching of Christ, the creative power of God, through whom alone salvation can come. The conclusion therefore is that the Gospel is the revelation of Jesus Christ in men, and the preaching of it is the making known to men of the possibility of Christ dwelling in them. Salvation is only by the power of God, and wherever the power of God is, there is salvation. Christ's salvation comes through the cross; therefore the cross of Christ is the power of God. The preaching of Christ and Christ crucified, is the preaching of the Gospel.

Mankind is accepted by God through His Son. We have redemption through Christ, His blood, forgiveness of our sins, according to the riches of His Grace, in whom we have trusted after we heard the word of Truth, the Gospel of our salvation, in whom we believed. The Gospel involves an inheritance; in fact the mystery of the Gospel is really the possession of the inheritance, for in Christ we have obtained an inheritance.

What are the people of God inheritance too? Heb 1:2—"heirs of all things." —Rev 21:7—"He that overcometh shall inherit all things." The Son of God was not recognized as such, by the world; therefore the world knows not Christians because it knew not Christ! The world today will not know the Christian because the world know's not Christ

Mankind by creation is a son of God; but through sin he became a child of wrath, a child of Satan, to whom he rendered obedience, instead of to God.

We are told in Isa 52:3—"that we have sold ourselves for nought; and we shall be redeemed without money." Thank our almighty for His Love, for His willingness to allow His Son to come to this world, that God, Himself created for man to enjoy and love, and die for our sins. Heb 9:28—"Christ was once offered to bear the sins of many; and unto them that look for Him shall appear the second time without sin unto salvation." Christ bore the curse of the law for us. What is this "curse"? John 7:49 —"This people who know not the law is cursed." Galatians 3:10—"Cursed is everyone who does not continue in all things which are written in the book of the Law, to do them."

Why is the Law of God such a conflict in the world today ?

We hear some say God changed His Law, but we know this is not true when in His Holy Word, "Malachi 3:6—"For I am the Lord, I change not." Again in Matt 5:17—"Jesus says, Think not that I came to destroy the Law." We have a promise in Ps 118:8—"It is better to trust in the Lord than to put confidence in man."

The Gospel does not deal exclusively in the future. It is for every day, present and future. Gal 3:29—"If we are Christ's, then we are Abraham's seed and heirs according to the promise." Of what are we heirs too? Rom 4:13—"For the promise, that he should be the heir of the world through the righteousness of faith." Every person is an heir of Christ, but we have to be willing to accept the promises of God. God is the Creator of all people, but God gave each person the choice to become His child ! God offers His riches freely to everyone, but no one can have any part in them except as he accepts Christ. Have you made your choice ?

To preach the Gospel, is to preach the Cross of Christ, and the Love of God to allow His Son to come to this earth and suffer and die for our sins on the cross. The penalty for the sins of every person that has ever been born. The choice is left to every person to accept this gift and to live according to the Law of Love "commandments". Have you made a choice? When you and I proclaim the Gospel and are attacked for our faith and hope, remember those who persecuted Christ, His disciples. Were they popular with the world? Some defend their silence that their faith is deeply private and don't want to force their faith on others. if you have decided to make Jesus your Lord and Saviour, then it makes sense to be publicly grateful. Don't be like some of the people when Jesus walked the earth. John 12:43—"For they loved the praise of men more than the praise of God."

What did Jesus say about those who wanted to be known as Christians while He was on earth? "Woe to you Scribes and Pharisees, hypocrites ! For you cleanse the outside of the cup and of the plate, but inside they are full of extortion and rapacity. For you are like whitewashed tombs, which appear beautiful, but within they are full of dead men's bones and all uncleanness. You also outwardly appear righteous to men, but within you are full of hypocrisy and iniquity. Yet there was 'tears'in the voice of Jesus as He uttered His rebukes to those who wanted to be known as Christians. Are their people today like this ? Jesus declares that the open sinner is less guilty than he who professes to serve God, but who bears no fruit. The Pharisees made void the Law of God by teaching for doctrines the commandments of men. Does this go on today?

When Jesus announced He was the Messiah of prophecy in 'Isa 49:8,9' and Isa 61:1,2, to the people in Nazareth, the church He attended "Luke 4:16-24. Christ was not accepted then and many today do not accept Jesus Christ the Saviour of mankind. Read what the people did to Jesus when He read to them from the Scripture, the prophecy of Himself. Luke 4:28-30. Jesus did not attend church there again. Do we see the same today, that people will not accept Jesus, the only One who can save them? The truth is never popular with the sinners who seek not the truth.

Scripture says that there was nothing about Jesus while He was on earth that men should desire Him. In other words, He was entirely human in every way. Jesus worked hard as a carpenter's Son and as a carpenter until He was thirty years old, providing the means of living for Himself and His mother. While growing up we can see from the way people reacted to Him that they did not see in Him any outwardly compelling reason to believe that He was any different from any other man. Jesus was unable to rely upon any resource that was within Himself, for He sought strength from His Father in prayer. He knew He could sin. He risked all to come here, and in order to be victorious, He stayed close to the

Father in heaven. His encounter with Satan in the wilderness was not a fake or a mockery. It was a real temptation, a genuine test.

The everlasting Gospel is the preaching of Christ, the creative power of God, through whom alone salvation can come! The conclusion therefore is that the Gospel is the revelation of Jesus Christ in men, and the preaching of it is the making known to men of the possibility of Christ dwelling in them. Salvation is only by the power of God, and wherever the power of God is, there is salvation. Christ's salvation comes through the cross; therefore the cross of Christ is the power of God. So the preaching of Christ and Christ crucified is the preaching of the Gospel.

Mankind is accepted by God through His Son. We have redemption through Christ, His blood, forgiveness of our sins, according to the riches of His Grace, in whom we have trusted after we heard the word of truth, the Gospel of our salvation, in whom we believed. The Gospel involves an inheritance; in fact the mystery of the Gospel is really the possession of the inheritance, for in Christ we have obtained an inheritance.

What are the people of God heirs too? "Heb 1:2"—says "heirs of all things." Rev 21:7—"He that overcometh shall inherit all things." The Son of God was not recognized as such, by the world; therefore the world knoweth not Christians because it knew not Christ! The world will not know the Christian today because the world knows not Christ.

Mankind by creation is a son of God; but through sin he became a child of wrath, a child of Satan, to whom he rendered obedience instead of to God. We are told in Isa 52:3—"that we have sold ourselves for nought; and we shall be redeemed without money." Thank our almighty for His love, for His willingness to allow His Son to come to this world, that God, Himself created for man to enjoy and love, and die for our sins. Heb 9:28-"Christ was once offered to bear the sins of many; and unto them that look for Him shall appear the second time without sin unto salvation." Christ bore the curse of the law for us. What is this "Curse". John 7:49 says "This people who know not the law is cursed." Galatians 3:10-"Cursed is everyone that continue not in all things which are written in the book of the law to do them."

We can read what Jesus preached [Gospel] while His time on earth in Matt 5:2—12, and verses 17—19. Jesus taught the Beatitudes and told everyone that He came not to destroy the Law or the Prophets. Jesus said that "till heaven and earth pass away, one jot or one tittle will by no means pass from the Law till all is fulfilled. Other teachings of Jesus are in Matt 7:1 "don't judge." Other things He taught V-13 wide is the gate and broad is the way that leads to destruction. V-23, 24, Matt 12:9, V-37, Luke 24:27—"And beginning at Moses and all the prophets, He expounded unto them in all the scriptures, the things concerning Himself." What would Jesus say to people today? Jesus told the people "Matthew 15:8" -"This people draweth nigh unto Me with their mouth, and honoureth Me with their lips; but their heart is far from Me." V-9—"But in vain they do worship Me, teaching for doctrines the commandments of men."

Mark 1:14—15— tells that Jesus after He was baptized went to Galilee "preaching the gospel of the kingdom of God." V-16— 'THE TIME IS FULFILLED, and the kingdom of God is at hand; repent ye, and believe the gospel."

Paul says in Rom 1:16—The Gospel is the power of God to salvation for everyone that believes. Galatians 1:6-7 tells that some are called into another gospel, which is not another but, some would pervert the gospel of Christ. We all know this to be true today, we only need to notice all the different names in front of our Churches. But which one teaches the Gospel of Christ ? Remember, we are not saved because we belong to a Church. We are saved when we are committed to Christ and each person has to stand alone as there were not another person in the world. If you do not hear what Christ preached while on the earth from your Pastor, read for yourself from God's Holy Bible. We don't need to think the Gospel has changed for our day and time, for we read in Scripture [Isa 31:2]— "He will not call back His words." [Eccl 3:14}—"I know that all God does will last forever; there is no adding to it or taking from it." The Word of God is a comfort to read and know, we don't need to worry about what has changed ! What's now will be forever in His word for our salvation !

The Gospel is a message of peace and love. Christianity is a system which, when received and obeyed would spread peace, harmony, and happiness throughout the earth. The Gospel of Christ will unite in close brotherhood all who accept it's teachings. It was the mission of Jesus to reconcile men to God, and thus to one another. The Gospel is the message that brings joy, hope, and salvation from sin. The Gospel is a message for all people. How do we know ? John 3:16- tells- "For God so loved the world, that He gave His only begotten Son, that whosoever believes in Him should not perish, but have everlasting life."

Our first duty is to study our Bible, we should always pray before we open God's Word for understanding. We may think it strange that the leaders did not know about the time when Christ came in their day. yet, many today fail in the very same way the Jew's of Christ's day failed. We fail to study and believe the prophecies just like the Jews.

During the first twenty-five hundred years of human history, there was no written revelation of the Gospel. The written Word began in the time of Moses. Jewish tradition ascribes the first five books of the old Testament, the work to Moses. The Bible points to God as its Author, yet it was written by human hands, The ten commandments were written by God Himself and spoken to the people of Israel Himself.

There is a strange and solemn power in the words of Scripture that speak directly to the hearts of those who are longing for Truth. Truth is the voice of God, and will carry conviction to those who hear and study the Gospel of truth. Christians today are to be the salt of the earth. Matt 5:13—"Ye are the salt of the earth." How can that be? We should make others thirsty for the Word of God !

What does the Gospel consist of ? The Gospel is the good news of salvation through Christ and Him crucified, for the Gospel is the power of God unto salvation. The doctrine of the second advent is the very keynote of the Sacred Scripture. The Gospel is the record of this world and all that was made and by Whom and how it was made. John 1:1-14 "In the beginning was the Word, and the Word was with God, and the word was God. All things were made by Him, and without Him was not anything made that was made. —He was in the world, and the world was made by Him, and the world knew Him not. He came unto His own, and His own received Him not. But as many as received Him, to them He gave power to become the sons of God." The Gospel involves an inheritance, in fact the mystery of the Gospel is really the possession of the inheritance, for in Christ we have obtained an inheritance.

OFFERINGS AND TITHE'S

Is Offering's and Tithe's part of the Gospel ? Why should we pay Tithe ? The paying of tithe-[10 per/cent] of our income is not a Jewish or Levitical ordinance. Long before Levi was born, Abraham paid tithe. He paid them to Melchizedek, whose priesthood is the Christian priesthood. We are not told when it was first made known to man, but we see that it was well known in the days of Abraham. Gen 14:18—"Then Melchizedek King of Salem brought out bread and wine; he was the Priest of God Most High. Why and do Christians need to be concerned about tithe? We read in "Acts 16:17" These men—preacher's— are the "servants of the Most High God","," who proclaim to us the way salvation." These statements reveal the source of how to support God's work, to make known the Gospel.

When you and I believe God's word, it is counted for righteousness. Why? Because faith means building upon God and His Word, and that means the receiving of the life of God and His Word. [1 Cor 9:14]—"the Lord commanded that those who preach the Gospel should live from the Gospel." This is the means to support the pastors of the Gospel. Paul says in V-16—"Woe is me if I do not preach the Gospel." What will pastors say when Christ comes that have preached their own gospel, and not the Gospel from God's Holy Word ? When you and I believe God's Word, it is counted for righteousness. Why? Because faith means building upon the Word of God and is counted for righteousness. Christians will support the giving of the Tithe to support giving the gospel to the world.

Malachi 3:8-10—"Will a man rob God. Yet you have robbed Me! but you say, In what way have we robbed You? In tithes and offerings. You are cursed with a curse, For you have robbed Me, Even this whole nation. Bring all the tithes into the storehouse. That there may be food in My house. And try Me now in this, says the Lord of Hosts. "If I will not open for you the windows of heaven And pour out for you such blessing that there will not be room enough to receive it." So many people do not trust in what our Lord says, and choose their own ways in serving God. Why?

Some might say they cannot afford to pay tithe. God looks upon those that are rich and those that are poor alike. God is no respecter of persons. God looks upon the heart. Jesus was born among the poor. Give back to God of your entrusted possessions and more will be entrusted to you. Keep your possessions to yourself, and you will receive no reward in this life, and will lose the reward of the life to come. What God blesses is blessed. Therefore "a little that a righteous man hath is better than the riches of many wicked"-Ps 37:16. Prov 3:9-10 "Honor the Lord with all thy substance, and with the first fruits of all thine increase, so shall thy barns be filled with plenty, and thy presses shall burst out with new wine "Proverbs 3:9-10. I . Matt 6:21 "For where your treasure is, there will your heart be also." What will pastors say when Christ comes that have preached their own gospel, and not from God's Holy Word ? When people believe and honor God's Holy Word, it is counted for righteousness.

IS THE GOSPEL
WRITTEN IN STONE?

MATT 7:24—"Whoever hearth these sayings of Mine, and doeth them, I will liken him unto a wise man, which built his house upon a rock." Jesus while on earth and while speaking to a crowd of people, common people and some of the chief priest and Pharisees said Matt 21:42-45 "The stone—"Jesus"—which builders rejected, the same has become the head of the corner; this is the Lord's doing, and it is marvelous in our eyes? [V-44] "Whosoever shall fall on this stone shall be broken, but whosoever it shall fall, it will grind him to powder."

Those who believe in the Gospel will be saved and those who don't accept the Gospel will suffer the destruction of God when He comes. Faith means building upon God's Word—1 Peter 2:5 We are lively stones when we build upon God's Word, acceptable to God by Jesus Christ. Ps 92:15-"the Lord is upright; He is my rock, and there is no unrighteousness in Him." Therefore, since faith means to build upon God and His Holy Word, it is self—evident that faith means to build upon His Holy Word. It is said that faith must be righteousness to the one who possesses and exercises it. No righteousness will be of any worth at the appearing of Christ except that which is through the faith in Christ—Phil 13:9. WE ARE GIVEN A PROMISE IN REV 2:17—"To him that overcomes, I will give him a white stone, and on that stone a new name written which no one knows except him who receives it." Our Lord has a new name for each one who loves Him.

2 Corinthians 13:8- "We can do nothing against the truth,

but for the Truth." Are the traditions of man more worthy of faith than the Gospel of our Saviour? It was the Love of God for man that prompted Him to express His will in the ten commandments, God's Law has ten simple laws, four which points man to God, our supreme love to God, and the last six commandments to our love for our fellow men.

We hear so many, who are deceived by the enemy constantly claiming, 'I am saved'; but they show such contempt of God's Law of righteousness and know nothing of saving Grace. Will our Lord take to heaven men and women who have no respect for His law of the universe ? What is to bring the sinner to the knowledge of his sins unless we know the word of God given in [1 John 3;4]. "Sin is the transgression of the Law." the Gospel without the Law is inefficient and powerless. The Law and the Gospel are a perfect whole. The law of God produce love and faith unfeigned.

Hosea 4:6,—"My people are destroyed for lack of knowledge, Because you have rejected knowledge, I will also reject thee— because thou hast forgotten the Law of thy God, I will also forget thy children." — V-2"By swearing and lying, and killing, and stealing, and committing adultery, they break out restraint, with bloodshed upon bloodshed." This is the result of banishing the Gospel of God.

From the beginning of mankind, 'Cain and Able and those who honor the Word of God as the only rule of life, and hollow the Law of God, have been branded as heretics. Why? Because they do not follow the traditions of man. It is never safe to follow the majority of people. What happened to the majority in the time of Noah and the flood ? Is it safe to follow the majority today? Our lives today need to be founded upon the Word of God, which is the only true system for the Christian following the Gospel of God.

The Bible is an anvil that has worn out many hammers. "The word of God stands forever" "All His commandments are sure. They stand fast forever and ever, and are done in truth and uprightness." Isa 40:8; Ps 111:7-8. Whoever builds upon the authority of man will be overthrown; but that which is founded upon the rock of God's immutable word shall stand forever.

Every nation on earth has it's laws, which command respect and obedience; no government could exist without them; and can it be conceived that our Creator of the heavens and the earth has no law to govern the beings He has created ? Suppose prominent ministers were to publicly teach that the statutes which govern our land and protect the rights of its citizens were not obligatory—that they restricted the liberties of the people, and therefore ought not be obeyed; how long would such men be tolerated in the pulpit ? Is it a graver offense to disregard the laws of states and nations than to trample upon the law of God which is the foundation of all governments?

It would be more consistent for the nations to abolish their statutes and laws, and permit people to do as they please than for the Ruler of the Universe to annul His Law and leave the world without a standard to condemn the guilty or justify the obedient. Would we know the result of making void the Law of God ? The experiment has been tried. Terrible were the scenes enacted in France when atheism became the controlling power. It has been demonstrated to the world that to throw off restraints which God has imposed, is to accept the rule of the cruelest of tyrants. When the standard of righteousness is set aside, the way is open for the prince of evil to establish his power in the earth. Those who teach people to regard lightly the commandments of God, sow disobedience to reap disobedience. God forbids dishonest practices, coveting, lying and defrauding. Men are ready to trample upon His statutes as a hindrance to there worldly prosperity; but the results of banishing God's precepts will be such as they do not anticipate.

GOD'S TRUTH

THE WORD OF GOD is the Gospel of Truth ! Some today are lacking faith in the Word of God, as the wife of Abraham did when she told her husband to go to her maid to raise up her a child. She thought she had faith, and even Abraham thought carrying out her advice, he would be in harmony with the word of the Lord. They both reasoned that God had promised them a large family. Thus today it is human reason that man deals with the Word of God. We know that later, both Abraham and his wife fully believed the Lord. Heb 11:11—Through faith also Sarah herself received strength to conceive seed, and was delivered of a child when she was past age, because she judged Him faithful who had promised.

Faith and Spiritual things are not imaginary things. That which is spiritual is more real than that which is fleshly, because only that which is spiritual will endure forever ! Therefore, if Abraham had only relied on the words of the Lord, instead of hearkening to the voice of his wife, he might have saved much trouble later.

The lesson of Abraham and Sarai, is a lesson for all mankind today. Recorded in John 8, Jesus tells people; "If ye abide in My word, then are ye My disciples; and ye shall know the truth, and the truth shall make you free." People today as well as then say they are not in bondage to anyone. Jesus says "Everyone that committeth sin is the bondservant of sin." The sum of the matter is that in the promise to Abraham, there is the Gospel; and any attempt to make the promises apply to any other than those who are Christ's is an attempt to nullify the promises of the Gospel of God.

God made a covenant with Abraham, and this covenant also includes all people who today accept the Gospel. This covenant with Abraham includes all people who today accept the Gospel. This covenant includes everlasting life. The "Word" of Truth is the Gospel of Salvation. When we believe the Gospel, we are sealed by the Holy Spirit, and that seal is the pledge of assurance to our inheritance, until it is bestowed at the coming of Christ. We know that sometimes we fail as Abraham did, and he repented and turned to the Lord again in full faith. When we fail or sin, we must repent and ask the Lord to help us to be faithful to His Word of Truth, the Gospel.

When we accept the Gospel and believe the truth of God's Word, we are not exempt from trials and temptations of Satan. We will more so be a focus for Satan's temptations. Satan will put doubts to our mind, and no man is good enough to be free from the suggestion's of Satan. Even Jesus was tempted Himself even as each one on earth is today. Heb 4:15—"He was tempted in all points like as we are, yet without sin." It is not "sin" to be tempted by Satan in our ears, but acting upon his temptations is sin.

Friendship with Christ is the complete trust in His Word, and friendship is based upon mutual confidence. Isa 51:7—"Hearken unto Me, ye that know righteousness, the people in whose heart is My Law; fear ye not the reproach of men, neither be ye afraid of their reviling!"

Do you think it would make no difference with the Lord if you were lost, because you are so obscure and insignificant? Your worthiness or unworthiness has nothing what so ever to do with the matter. The Lord says, "I, even I am He that blotteth out thy transgressions for Mine own sake, and I will not remember thy sins."-Isa 43:25. Christ swore by Himself to save all that come to

Him through Jesus Christ. Think about it; God pledged Himself and His own existence, to our salvation in Jesus Christ. God shows our true value; but we are to be redeemed without money, even by the precious blood of Jesus Christ. It would be a sad loss to you if you should fail of salvation; but it would be a far greater loss if you should fail through any fault of God.

Through one man's, sin death came into the world. Satan is the adversary of all that is Holy, and good. "The last enemy of man shall be destroyed, it is death"— I Cor 15:22—26. "But If the spirit of Him that raised up Jesus from the dead dwells in you, He that raised up Christ from the dead shall also quicken your mortal bodies by His Spirit that dwelleth in you."— Rom 8:11.

We hear many today claiming to be saved, but they show such contempt of God's rule of righteousness and know nothing of God's saving Grace. The heart is not in harmony with the Law of God, but is at enmity with the Law of God which is the rule for all the universe. Will our Lord take to heaven men and women who have no respect for the Law of His universe ?

No one will be lost because of their sins. Our sins were paid for at the Cross. Those that are lost will be because they refused pardon. When we turn our back on Jesus Christ, we are lost.

Many will be like a young man who could have been set free from death row, but he refused to accept the one person who could pardon his sentence of death.

"True Story":

A young man who lived in a western state had never done anything very wrong. But while playing a game of cards he lost his temper. Picking up a revolver, he shot and killed his opponent. He was arrested and tried and sentenced to hang.

Because of the wonderful life he had lived previously, his

relatives and many friends got up a petition for him. It seemed as though everyone wanted to sign it, and people all over the state eagerly signed.

At last it was taken to the Governor, who happened to be a Christian, and tears came to his eyes as he looked at the large basket filled with petitions. He decided to pardon, he put it in his pocket, then dressed in the garb of a clergyman, he made his way to the prison.

As the governor approached the young man's death cell the young man sprang to the bars; "Get out of here" he cried, I don't want to see you. I have had enough religion at home. Seven of your kind have visited me already." but the governor interrupted, "Wait a moment, young man; I have something for you. Let me talk to you." Listen, exclaimed the young man in anger, If you don't get out of here at once I'll call the guard and have you put out ! But young man, continued the governor, I have news for you—the very best. Won't you let me tell you about it? You heard what I said, replied the young man, and if you don't leave immediately I'll call the warden.

Very well, replied the Governor, and with a sad heart the Governor turned and left. In a few moments the warden approached, "Well, young man, I see you had a visit from the Governor." "What" cried the young man. Was that the man dressed in a garb of a clergyman the Governor? Yes, he was replied the warden, and he had a pardon in his pocket for you, but you would not listen to him.

Get me a pen, ink and paper, cried the young man. And sitting down, he wrote, "Dear Governor, I owe you an apology. I am sorry for the way I treated you————and so on.

The Governor received the letter, turned it over, and wrote on the back, "No longer interested in this case." The day came for the young man to die. Is there anything you want to say before you die, he was asked. "Yes", he answered, tell the young men of America that I am not dying for my crime—I am not dying because I am a murderer. The Governor pardoned me. I could have lived. Tell them, that I am dying because I did not accept the Governor and his pardon."

No one will be lost because of their sins. That was paid for by Jesus at the cross. If anyone is lost it will be because he or she has refused pardon. It is no longer a sin-issue, it is the "Son" issue. When we come to the place where we turn our back on Jesus Christ and His Law, we are lost. It's our relationship with the One who has given us pardon from our sins that will determine future life !

LAMBS POINTING TO CHRIST

As we know and read about all the lambs sacrificed before Christ came the first time, that pointed to the coming of Christ, which pointed to when the Lamb of God-Jesus Christ, would come and be sacrificed for mankind sins. There was a big difference—None of the lambs sacrificed ever was raised to life again. These lambs pointed to the time when Christ would come willing to be give His life for our sins. The sacrifice of Lambs ended at the Cross. This is why today our hope is in Jesus Christ, for He died for our sins, in our place.

Many people today must think like the wife of Abraham and like Jacob, that the Lord needs help. They thought they could work out the promises of God in their own way. They forgot the promises of God was wholly in the Lord's power. No person can have anything to do with the disposing of God's blessings, except to reject it for themselves.

God chooses men not for what they are, but for what He can make of them. There is no limit to what God can make of even the meanest and depraved person, if they are willing, and believe His Word, the Gospel ! A gift can not be forced upon one, and therefore one has to be 'willing' to receive God's righteousness. God can do exceeding abundantly above all that we ask or think, if we but believe His Word—Gospel—which effectually works in them that believe.

Scripture reveals how the respectable people—"Pharisees"— were more highly honored than the publicans and harlots, and yet Christ said that these would go into the Kingdom before they did.

The reason was that the Pharisees trusted in themselves for their salvation, and disbelieved God, while the publicans and harlots believed the Lord.

Scripture tells that God preached the "Gospel" to Abraham in the words "In thee shall all the families of the earth be blessed." And again God spoke the Gospel to Jacob, "In thee and in thy seed shall all the families of the earth be blessed." God is preaching the same Gospel to each today ! The Gospel is summed up in two word's- Repentance and Faith. We are told "without faith it is impossible to please God." God calls men to His work, not because they are perfect, but in order that He may give them the necessary training for it.

Think of Moses, whom God raised up to free Israel. Moses was raised up to believe he would be used of the Lord to deliver Israel from the bondage of Egypt. As Moses was visiting his brethren and seeing one of them suffer wrong. Moses defended him. The Lord designed that the people should be delivered by the hand of Moses, but this was not the way our Lord had planed. Moses attempt to deliver Israel was a complete failure. The people and Moses did not understand that the Lord does not use— "force"— in the fellowship of working for those who love Him. The natural thought then, as now, was that the only way to secure rights, was to meet force with force. Man's way is not God's way; and God's way is the only right way.

We are told in James 5:7-8, "Be patient therefore, brethren, unto the coming of the Lord,— Be ye also patient; establish your hearts; for the coming of the Lord draweth nigh."

DID CHRIST PREACH THE GOSPEL WHILE CHRIST WAS THIS EARTH?

The strongest proof of the Divinity of Christ mission was that the Gospel was preached to the poor. [Matt 11:5]—"The blind received their sight, and the lame walked, the lepers were cleansed, and the deaf hear, the dead are raised up, and the poor have the Gospel preached to them." Jesus knew the needs of the poor as no other ever can, and His remedy was the Gospel. The right understanding of the inheritance which the Gospel promises can alone make man patient under earthy oppression. For three years the Lord of light and glory went among the people, doing good and healing all that was oppressed of the Devil. Christ warned the people while on earth and people today—Matt 23:37; John 5:40—"Ye will not come to Me, that ye might have life." Christ leaves that choice to each person then, and for us today. Why? The Kingdom of God is and will always be a kingdom of love. Jesus was willing to pour out His soul unto suffering and death, to bring salvation within our reach; but few come to Him that they might have eternal life.

The great sin of the Jews was their rejection of Jesus Christ, the great sin of Christians today is their rejection of the Law of God, the foundation of His government in heaven and earth. Every transgression of the Law of God, is a seed sown which yields its unfailing harvest.

Faith in Christ does not assure any person an earthly possession. Those who are heirs of God are poor of this world, but rich in faith. Christ Himself had not a place of His own on this earth, where He could lay His head; therefore none need think that following Christ in Truth will insure them worldly possessions. It is more likely to be the contrary

James 2:5—"God has chosen the poor of this world, rich in faith, and heirs of the kingdom of Truth, who will hear His voice, "Open ye the gates, that the righteous nation which keeps the Truth may enter in." Isa 26:2. Faith is the evidence of things not seen. People today that honor and Love the Gospel of Truth are the people of a living Faith. Yet we are told in —1 Cor 10:12—"Therefore let him that thinks he stands, take heed lest he fall."

Jesus preached the Gospel to the poor and to those who came to Him. What did He preach and teach? We are told in Matt 13:13-15 what Jesus taught the people, "I speak to them in parables —-because they do not understand. What did Jesus preach to the people? Matt 15:6-9 "You have made the commandments of God of no effect by your tradition." "These draw near Me with their mouth and honor Me with their lips, but their hearts are far from Me. In vain they worship Me, teaching as doctrine the commandments of men." V-14 "let them alone, they are blind leaders of the blind, both will fall in the ditch." Jesus told His disciples Matt 16:12 "beware of the doctrines of the Pharisees." What would Jesus say today about all the different names on the front of our Churches and what is taught by them ?

Some preachers think they should be called Father because they are the leader of the people. What does Scripture say about calling someone 'Father'? Matt 23:9 answers this, "Do not call anyone on earth your "Father" for One is your Father, He who is in heaven."

When Jesus walked this earth there were many who taught different gospels just as today. What did Jesus say about these different teachers of the Gospel ? Luke 6:40 "a teacher is not above his teacher, but anyone who is perfectly trained will be like his teacher." Luke 9:26—"For who ever is ashamed of Me and My words. of him the Son of Man will be ashamed when He comes in His Father's glory, and with the Holy angels." Luke 16:13—"no servant can serve two masters ! Jesus said while on earth." Luke 21:33—"Heaven and earth shall pass away; but My words shall not pass away." Jesus had a message for the people while on earth and for people today. We find this message in John 8:51—"Most assuredly, I say to you, if anyone keeps My word, he shall never see death." Then why do people die on this earth today? People do not understand death, Jesus calls death 'sleep'! Why? Dan 12:2—"Everyone found written in the book, and many of those who sleep in the dust of the earth shall awake to everlasting life, and some to shame and everlasting contempt." Jesus said that Lazarus sleeps, but He would go wake him up—John 11:11 & V14— these things Jesus said, "Lazarus is dead." We can read other text about death and sleep—1 Thess 4:15-17; For the Lord Himself will descend from heaven with a shout, with the voice of an archangel and the dead in Christ will rise first. Then we who are alive and remain shall be caught up together with them in the clouds to meet the Lord in the air, and thus we shall be with the Lord."

Many people believe they go to heaven to be with the Lord as soon as they die, or some say that their soul goes to be with the Lord. When God breathed into man, man became a living soul, there is a difference and man has not understood what is a soul. All mankind will either go with Christ when Christ comes to gather those who are living and those who are sleeping in the graves to heaven to be with the Lord forever, or the unbelievers and the wicked will be destroyed by the brightness of Christ coming and will rest for a thousand years while the righteous search the records to see why some are not saved.

Jesus Christ comes to gather those who love Him and obey His Law, and will live with Him for eternity. God wants all to be saved but He leaves the choice to each person. Why? Because the kingdom of God is a Kingdom that is ruled by Love. No force is used in the kingdom of God on this earth or will be used in God's kingdom in heaven and the new earth. Does that sound like a kingdom you would like to be part of?

Faith in Christ does not assure any person an earthly possession. Those who are heirs of God are poor of this world, but rich in faith. Christ Himself had not a place of His own on this earth, where He could lay His head; therefore none need think that following Christ in Truth will insure them worldly possessions. It is more likely to be the contrary.

WHAT IS THE GOSPEL TODAY?

The message of salvation has been preached in all ages. The Gospel message today is part of the Gospel that could be proclaimed only in the last days. Daniel 12:4—"many shall run to and fro and knowledge shall be increased." 2 Thess 2:3-"let no man deceive you by any means; for that day shall not come, except there come a falling away first, and that man of sin be revealed, the son of perdition." Scripture does not say the day or hour should be known, He gave us signs, in order that we may know at least the approach of His coming.

Jesus and the Gospel, is not the most popular person or subject around to get a conversation started. Was Jesus popular among the leaders of the people and the Church when He was on earth? Are people popular today that share the gospel of Truth in God's Word? While Jesus walked among men, the religious people of that day accused Jesus of —Luke 23:5—"He stirs up the people, teaching throughout all Judea," Are people today accepted any better ?

We see prophecy being fulfilled all over the world today, Why? Around the towns and cities we see people killing people, Why ? 1 Chron 10:13—"because of the unfaithfulness to the Lord, because of not keeping the Lord's commandments, His eternal Law. People disregard God's Law and God does not interfere to protect the property of those who transgress His Law, breaking His covenant with them. God is Love, not force ! No one can love God supremely and transgress one of His commandments. What evidence have we that we have pure love without alloy ?

God created a standard —His Law of Commandments— John 14:21—"He that hath My commandments, and keepeth them, he it is that loves Me."

Confusion fills the world. So what are we hearing in our Churches today? Many claim that a position of the church gives them authority to dictate what others believe and what they should do. This claim God does not sanction. Upon no finite being can we depend for guidance. The history of Israel is a warning to our churches today. Our profession of faith is not a guarantee in this day, but the state of our affections. Do we love to talk about Jesus Christ, of the home which Christ has prepared for them that love and obey Him? Whom will you and I believe, the leaders of the different churches of the world or the Word of God. Will we follow the traditions of the world for Truth or the Word of God in Scripture ? We can't wait till Christ comes to make that decision. We don't know when our life might end and Christ will know before He comes who Loves Him enough, we are in the testing time today not later ! Probation will end before Christ comes, make your decision today, when Jesus comes it will be to late !

All the Gospel is summed up in God's Law of Commandments. Jesus told all the people while on this earth—John 14:15—"If you love Me, keep My commandments." God has proven His Love for you and me while on the Cross and died for everyone's sins. Many receive the Gospel with joy at first, but as soon as persecution and ridicule arise they become offended. We read in Acts 14:22—"We must through much tribulation enter into the kingdom of God." And those who do enter in must learn to rejoice even in tribulation. We are not promised that we will be accepted by the majority, neither was the Gospel excepted by the majority in Noah's time or when God wanted to save the people of Israel in Egypt. Even after God saved Israel through the waters as Pharaoh wanted to destroy them. The people then after God saving them through the water, did not trust God. The people then had to spend 40 years in the wilderness, because the people did not trust God. If only then the people had put their trust in God, they could have had a life of plenty. Are we people today any different? Does Christian people put their trust in the Gospel or do we trust what comes out of the mouth of other people? Israel did not trust what God wanted them to do, and they suffered and died in the wilderness before they got to the promised land. Do we today do the same? Why not get the Truth of God, the Gospel of God from His Word in Scripture? Rom 15:4—"For whatsoever things were written before time, were written for our learning, that we through patience and comfort of the scriptures might have hope." 2 Tim 3:16-17.—"All scripture is given by inspiration of God, and is profitable for doctrine, for reproof, for correction, for instruction in righteousness:" V-17—"That the man of God may be perfect, throughly furnished unto every good works."

God wants all His creation to know the Truth-"Gospel". God is no respecter of persons, all that fear Him and "love" Him, is accepted -Acts 10:34-35.—"'In every nation whoever fears Him and works righteousness is accepted by Him." This is not new today, but has been true for ever, because He is always the same. Rom 4:11—"There is neither Jew nor Greek, there is neither bond nor free, there is neither male nor female, for we are all one in Christ Jesus—and heirs according to the promise." 2 Peter 3:9—"God is not willing that any should perish, but that 'all' should come to repentance." 1 Tim 2:4—He desires all men to be saved, and come to the knowledge of the truth." Eek 33:11—"As I live saith the Lord God, I have no pleasure in the death of the wicked; but that the wicked turn from his way and live." All people are God's people and belong to Him, His great Love embraces us all, without respect to race or nationality. We are told in Jer 1:5—"Before I formed you in the womb I knew you; before you were born, I sanctified you." Our Creator God wants everyone to know that He loves us enough to carry our sins to the cross and die for each person, but we have to make a choice to accept His love and His sacrifice for our sins. If we believe, and honor His Holy Word, we will honor His Law that all the other worlds honor.

Many believe the Law of commandments were given only to Israel at Sinai. but we can read in Rom 5:13-14, For until the Law sin was in the world, but sin is not imputed when there is no Law." Adam and Eve sinned and to know what sin is we only need to read -1 John 3:4—"whoever commits sin also commits lawlessness, and sin is lawlessness." The Law of God is a Law of Love, and God wants all people to honor His Law of Love. All those who wish to be saved will love God and keep His commandments. Ps 111:7-9—"The works of His hands are verity and justice.—They stand forever and ever, and are done in truth and uprightness—He has commanded His covenant forever."

There is a strange and solemn power in the words of Scripture that speaks directly to the hearts of those who are longing for truth. It is the voice of God, and it carries conviction to those who read and hear it. No one knows all the answers to everyone's questions, or all of the scriptures. If you know that God has made a change in your life, you have something to share with others. It was not the scholarly theologians who had an understanding of when Christ came.

IS THERE A FALSE GOSPEL IN THE CHRISTIAN CHURCHES TODAY?

The churches of our time are seeking aggrandizement and unwilling to see the prophecies that show that Christ is soon to come, as were the Jews at Christ first coming. The subject that Christ is coming is to be the wonderful theme kept before people today. The work of preaching the gospel has not been committed to the angels. it was not the scholarly theologians who had an understanding of Christ coming to earth to die for our sins.

Isa 5:21—"Woe to those who are wise in their own eyes." WHY ? V-24—"Because they have rejected the Law of the Lord of hosts, and despised the Word of the Holy One of Israel." Matt 7:21—23—"Not everyone who says to Me, 'Lord, Lord' shall enter the kingdom of heaven, but he who does the will of My Father in heaven. —Many will say to Me in that day, Lord, Lord, have we not prophesied in Your name, and cast out demons in Your name ?' And then I will declare to them, depart from Me, "you who practice lawlessness." Do you and I believe what Christ has said ? Is it safe to believe that any of the many churches preach God's Gospel ? Why not search the Scriptures for the Gospel Truth !

The line of distinction between professed Christians and the ungodly is now hardly distinguishable. Church members love what the world loves and are ready to join with them, and Satan determines to unite them in one body and thus strengthen his cause by sweeping all into the ranks of spiritualism. Protestants, and worldings will alike accept this form of godiness without the power.

It is important that the followers of Christ be different from the world. There are many preachers who say, "Oh, do as you please. It doesn't make any difference." Many churches never talk about these things or read the texts of Scripture that have to do with the way we dress and the way we eat and the way we live. But God condemns those who say that it makes no difference about all these things. Notice what God says about such preachers: "Her priests have done violence to My Law and have profaned My Holy things; they have made no distinction between the Holy and the common, neither have they taught the difference between the unclean and the clean, and they have disregarded My sabbaths, so that I am profaned among them." Ezekiel 22:26.

Some people say, but the contradictions of Christian doctrine are so confusing. One church says this, and another church says that. It's a puzzle to know what we should believe about the Sabbath and baptism and death and Christian standards of living and conduct." We need to look and read what our Creator did while on earth in the years He was on this earth. If we keep the Sabbath He kept, there's no problem there. If we believe what Jesus taught about death, it is simple and easy to understand. If we believe what Jesus taught about living separate from the world, there no problem. Christian doctrine will always be clear if we see it as it is in Jesus. What is going to count in the day when Christ comes is whether we have a relationship with Jesus that leads to obedience as naturally as fruit grows on a vine. We must be faithful to the Truth that God's Word has brought to us and love the Word of God, and do His commandments of love for during the great reformation, the 1800s, men like Marten Luther, John Wycliffe and others saw that the church had forsaken the Word of God for human tradition, and demanded that the Bible be restored to the people and its authority be established in the churches. Like the Pharisees of old, the great church had made the commandments of God of none effect by their traditions. The church proclaimed that people could purchase forgiveness with money. The claim resulted in injury to their cause, for it led many to the Bible to learn the truth for themselves. What did Peter of Scripture tell Simon Magus about purchasing the power of God in Acts 8:20—"Thy money perish with thee, because thou thought that the gift of God may be purchased with money?" Luther taught people that it is impossible for man, by his own works, to lesson his guilt or evade its punishment. Nothing but repentance to God and faith in Christ can save the sinner. It is clearly shown that the Gospel of Christ is the most valuable treasure of the church, and that the Grace of God, therein revealed, is freely bestowed upon all who seek it by repentance and faith. Wycliffe, like his Master, preached the gospel to the poor as well as on the streets of great cities and in the halls of the University. But his greatest work was the translation of the Scriptures into the English language. Wycliffe did more to break the fetters of ignorance and vice, more to liberate and elevate his country, than was ever achieved by the most brilliant victories on fields of battle. Wycliffe, proclaimed that the Gospel of Christ is the whole body of God's Commandments, the Law of heaven. and should I be silent he said—Never ! He declared the only true authority to be the voice of God speaking through His Word. He taught that the Bible is a perfect revelation of God's will, but the Holy Spirit is it's only interpreter, and every man is, by the study of its teachings, is to learn his duty for himself. Ps 119:130—"The entrance of your words gives light; it gives understanding to the simple."

Christians are not to follow others in their walk with the Lord, because the Gospel says both will fall in the ditch.—Matt 15:14. Why are we not to follow others who should be leaders for

Christians? Isa 5:24— explains—"Because they have rejected the Law of the Lord of hosts, and despised the Word of the Holy One of Israel." Isa 66:3—"Just as they have chosen their own ways, and their souls delight in their own ways." Jer 5:26—"for among My people are found wicked men," Jer 6:19—they have not heeded My words, nor My Law, but rejected it." We are reminded in Jer 8:9—they have rejected the Word of the Lord, So what wisdom do they have?" Jer 9:3—"they do not know Me; says the Lord." V-5— "They have taught their tongue to speak lies." V-6—"through deceit they refuse to know Me, says the Lord." Are the traditions of men more worthy of faith than the Gospel of our Creator God ?

Scripture warns Christians in Jer 12:6—"Do not believe them, even though they speak smooth words." Jer 14:14—The prophet prophecy lies in My name—they prophecy to you a worthless thing, and the deceit of their heart." God has given a warning to the leaders of His churches. Jer 48:10—"Cursed is he who does the work of the Lord deceitfully." 1 Tim 2:4-6—"The Lord desires all men to be saved and come to the knowledge of the Truth. For there is one God and one Mediator between God and man, the Man Christ Jesus." Be careful who you depend on for 'Truth' only believe what agrees with God's Gospel !

As our Lord warned Jeremiah about the leaders in his day, these warnings are good for Gods people today ! Jer 29:8-9—"Do not let your prophets and your diviners who are in your midst deceive you, nor listen to your dreams which you cause to be dreamed. For they prophesy falsely to you in My name. I have not sent them, says the Lord." This is still true today as well as then. Jer 23:16—"They speak of a vision of their own heart, not from the mouth of the Lord." Christians face the same conflict today as the people in Jeremiah's day. People were warned then and people need to be warned today.

Are people today different from Bible times? Eek 12:1-2—"son of man, you dwell in the midst of a rebellious house, which has eyes to see but does not see and ears to hear but does not hear; for they are a rebellious house." Eek 13:22—"Because with lies you have made the heart of the righteous sad, whom I have not made sad; and you have strengthened the hands of the wicked, so that he does not turn from his wicked way to save his life."

Our Lord has done what He can that all may know their Creator God. He gave us the Sabbath to be a sign between God and man, that we might know that our Creator God is our Creator who sanctifies us—Ezk 20:12. Yet in V13—we are told—"They rebelled against Me, —they profaned My Sabbaths." Why, we ask today has people turned away from God's Sabbath ? Hosea 10:13 [tells] "You have eaten the fruit of lies. Because you trusted in your own way." Zech 7:12—"Yes, they made their hearts like flint, refusing to hear the Law and the words which the Lord of Hosts had sent by His Spirit through the former prophets. Mal 2:8=9 "but you have departed from the way; You have caused many to stumble at the Law." —"Because you have not kept My ways, but have shown partiality in the Law." Many today are guilty as people in earlier times. We like to honor the parts of the Law that fits our life today. Christians should receive no other doctrines than those which rest on the Sacred Scriptures. Between truth and error there is an irrepressible conflict. To uphold and defend the one is to attack the other.

Jesus said to His disciples—John 15:18—"If the world hates you, you know that it hated Me before it hated you." The Truth is no more desired by the majority today than it was by the papists who opposed Martin Luther. Jesus reminded His disciples "Woe unto you, when all men speak well of you" ! Is the spirit of the world today, more in harmony with the Spirit of Christ than in earlier times? Are those who preach the Word of God in its purity, received with greater favor now, than then ?

The minister who has sacrificed 'truth' to gain favor will see and discern the character and influence of his teachings. Jer 23:1-2—"Woe be unto the pastors that destroy and scatter the sheep of My pasture—Behold I will visit upon you evil for your doings." Jer 25:34-35 "Wail, shepherds, and cry ! The shepherds will have no way to flee, Nor the leaders of the flock to escape." The setting aside of the divine precepts gave rise to the thousands of springs of evil, discord, hatred, iniquity, until the earth becomes one vast field of strife and corruption. What do we see today in all the nations of the world? The controversy between Satan and God, is now between men of the world and those who honor our Creator.

THE GOSPEL OF
FORGIVENESS OF SIN

If in our ignorance we make mistakes—sin—God does not leave us. Christ will never turn from one for whom He paid the ransom with His own life. Remember the thief on cross who asked our Lord to remember him when Jesus comes? Had he lived, he undoubtedly would have confessed his sins. But he didn't live, and we have no record of his confession. You remember the prodigal son who returned home? He had his confession memorized, but here we find one of the most beautiful interruptions in the whole Bible. The father meets his son, and takes him unto his home. Why didn't the father let his son confess? Because the father had forgiven his son already. These instances suggest that forgiveness is not based on our confession. God knows our heart better than we do. It is easy for us to think that our prayers are the basis for our forgiveness. But forgiveness is never based on our prayers. It ia based on Christ's prayer on the cross. "Father forgive them, for they know not what they do." This prayer of Christ for His enemies embraced the world. That isn't to say everyone accepts it, but it was granted. Forgiveness is not based upon our prayers; it is based upon Christ's prayer. Our Lord knows our heart better than we do. Romans 5:10—"While we were enemies, we were reconciled to God through the death of His Son." Forgiveness is provided through Christ; apart from any asking on our part. Each individual has to accept Christ before it effects our salvation. We must remember; "apostasy" is sin that needs to be confessed and asked to be forgiven. Apostasy is turning from Christ, saying

"Lord, I don't want you in my life." God honors our request but when we confess our sins and come to God, He is faithful and just to forgive.

But you ask, "What about the sins I commit after becoming a Christian? Do not these destroy my standing? We must remember that our Creator knows each person better than we know ourselves. What if a father or mother expelled his child every time he or she made a mistake, and not let them come back, until on their knees and say, "I'm sorry." If this is inconsistent at the human level, how incongruous must it be at the divine level. The idea that when we sin we suddenly become lost is purely of human devising. This must be part of Satan's instigations. No human parent would disown a child when the child disobeys.

What if we sin and five minutes later, we are killed. Must we be lost? If our salvation is based upon our misdeeds, we know that this is not the Gospel! The Gospel is good news, and our salvation is based upon Christ wholly and completely. Why then must we confess our sin if they are already forgiven? Very simple. To keep our hearts open that we may continue to receive God's forgiveness. What if I don't ask for God's forgiveness, what will happen to me? How often and many times can we continue to wound Christ and be sorry and receive God's forgiveness? Confession softens our heart.

An example of God's forgiveness is that of a little child who sneaks into his parents bedroom in the morning before they wake up, goes over to his father's trousers, slips his little hand into a pocket, pulls out a dime and quickly walks out. But the father was not asleep and saw his little boy take the dime. Now the father isn't going to go broke because he lost a dime, but he feels badly because of what his little son did. It is not the dime, it is the relationship. The father is hurt. Does he cease to love his son? Does he think, "He is no longer my son until he makes this right?" No. the father loves him even more. After a while, maybe hours, or days, the son begins to hurt. he feels terrible for what he has done, so he goes back to his father and, handing him the dime says, "Dad, I took this dime from you. I'm awfully sorry. Will you forgive me? The father puts his arm around his son saying, Son, I forgive you." Does the father mean that for the first time since his son took the dime he is now giving him forgiveness? No ! He had been forgiven all along. But the son now needs to be reminded. it needs to be pointed out. The father reminds his son of his love and forgiveness so that he don't have to become defensive about his mistakes. Our confession testifies that we have not spurned God's pardon. God can be just in forgiving our sins, something which He could not do if we didn't want it. The good news is that we are forgiven, that we live in complete pardon through Jesus Christ.

IS THE GOSPEL OF
GOD YOUR CHOICE!

God has provided for every person an opportunity to know that which will make him wise unto salvation. What will we do with this knowledge ?

Many today are of the same spirit as was Pharaoh, Ex 5:2— "Who is the Lord, that I should obey His voice ? The Gospel of God is simply what God has said, and recorded for all to know today. Every person on earth has the choice when we read or hear the Truth of God. When we read the record in Scripture about Pharaoh, who denied there was a Creator God, who said "Who is God"? But when the plagues began to come upon Egypt with interval's enough to allow Pharaoh to think. Pharaoh and his magicians could not stop the plagues, he had to admit there was a power greater than him and his magicians.

The same spirit today is manifested by people who refuse the Gospel of Truth and choose to believe the traditions of men, rather than the Gospel. The Gospel of Truth today is true as God's Word was to Pharaoh and Israel many years ago.

Jesus Christ is the Son of God, He is our Passover Lamb, the same as He was to the children of Israel in Egypt. Because, Jesus life is everlasting and indestructible, and those willing by faith to share the Truth, no one or the devil can take his life from him or us. 'Heb 13:8'—"Jesus Christ is the same yesterday and today and forever.

If only Christian people would read and study the Word of God, as they spend years in Universities to learn to be accepted for a position in the work place, they would be fitted for an eternity where there is no strife, sin, death, pain. The easy desire for an easy religion that requires no self-denial, no divorce from the follies of the world, has made the doctrine of faith only a popular doctrine. We hear from many people, we only need to believe and the blessing is yours. No other effort on the part of the receiver is supposed to be required. At the same time, they deny the authority of the Law of God, believing they are released from obligation to honor and keep God's commandments. What if that was all which was required for a Doctorate Degree today, only believe and you have eternal life ?

The desire for an easy religion that requires no striving, no self-denial, no divorce from the follies of the world, has made the doctrine of faith only a popular doctrine. What does the Gospel say ? James 2:14-24—"what doth it profit, my brethren, though a man say he hath faith, and have not works ? Can faith save him? —Even so faith, if it hath not works, is dead, being alone." V-19-"Thou believes that there is one God; thou doest well; the devils also believe, and tremble." V-20—"O vain man, that faith without works is dead." V-24—"Ye see then how that by works, a man is justified, and not by faith only. 1 John 4:1—"Beloved, believe not every spirit, but test the spirits, whether they are of God; because many false prophets are gone out into the world." We see this today in all the different sect and churches. Each believing they have the truth of the Gospel. Compare what is taught with Scripture. i John 2:3-5—"Now by this we know that we know Him, if we keep His commandments."—"He that saith I know Him, and keepeth not His commandments is a liar, and the truth is not in him. But who so keepeth His Word, in him verily is the love of God perfected; By this we know that we are in Him." Ps 1:1-3—"Blessed is the man that walks not in the council of the ungodly—But his delight is in the Law of the Lord—He shall be like a tree planted by the river of water."

How is your Christian walk with our Lord ? Are you just aiming for heaven? There is more to life than just aiming for heaven. You can know that victory is possible, because Jesus will help you in all that you do when you ask in faith. its hard to find a major character in the Bible who didn't have a testing season as part of their story. Noah faced the mockery of his community while building the Ark. Jacob struggled under the shadow of his brother. Joseph was sold into slavery by his own brothers and then betrayed by his master's wife in Egypt, only to be forgotten by those he helped while in prison. Just before Peter's fall, Christ said to him, Simon, behold, Satan hath desired to have you, that he may sift you as wheat." But the warning was resented. Peter declared confidently that he would never do what Christ had warned him against. "Lord", he said, "I am ready to go with thee to prison, and to death." His self confidence proved his ruin. He tempted Satan to tempt him, and he fell under the arts of the wily foe. Many today stand where Peter stood just before the cross in self-confidence. But those who trust in self are easily defeated. If we do not heed the cautions that God gives us, a fall is before us. We need to be able to say, "It is "written" to stand before the tempter and others for the protection of a "Thus saith the Lord."

No one is a hero at the beginning of their walk with God. David was anointed King, but waited 20 years for his reign as King to begin. He didn't force it to happen; he waited for God to make it happen. Following Christ is not a decision, we only make a choice. We choose whether to align with the Gospel of God or refuse to believe the Gospel.

Most people say they want to go to heaven, but they don't want to be with God, Why? Is this the same reasoning that Satan and some of the angels had ? Satan is good at hurting people, and then he frames God for it. What does Scripture say ? Don't be misled, my dear brothers and sisters. Whatever is good and perfect comes down to us from God our Father.

The Bible makes it clear that God does not enjoy to see people punished. The wicked to be destroyed is called God's strange act in Scripture. God wants to save every person, but leaves the choice to each person. Rebellion builds walls between God and us, Isa 59:2—"But your sins have separated you from your God, and your sins have hidden His face from you, so that He will not hear."

The Gospel of God is about love, His Love for mankind. If all we have and live for is each other, then we're in trouble. The Gospel Rev 3:20—"Behold, I stand at the door, and knock; If any man hear My voice and open's the door, I will come to him. We will share a meal together as friend's". Its time for people's walk to match their talks ! How do we do that ? The first thing to do is surrender to Christ. The next step is to let Christ guide you through the Scripture on what you need to do next. It is God who shields His creatures and hedges them from the power of the destroyer. Satan has control of all which God does not especially guard. Satan will favor and prosper some in order to further his own designs, and Satan will bring trouble upon others and lead men to believe that it is God who is afflicting them. Even now Satan is at work. In accidents and calamities by sea and by land, in great conflagrations, in tornadoes and hailstorms, fires, earthquakes, in every place and in thousands of forms. While Satan seeks to destroy those who honor God's law, Satan will cause them to be accused as lawbreakers which causes all the destruction that Satan causes.

Christians must remember that God does not use "force" or "fear" only "Love" to those who come to Him. Those who endeavor to obey all the commandments of God will be opposed and derided as the end of this world gets nearer to the end. It is not enough to have good intentions, it is not enough to do what a man thinks is right. Our soul's salvation is at stake, and we should search the Scriptures for ourselves. However strong may be our convictions, however confident we may be that the minister knows what is truth, this is not God's foundation, each person needs a foundation from God's Holy Bible. We know from the past, Jesus told people while on earth—Mark 12:24—"ye know not the Scriptures, neither the power of God." It's not enough to do what a man thinks is right or what the minister tells as truth ! Our soul's salvation is at stake. God has given us His Word that we may become acquainted with it's teachings and know for ourselves what He requires of us. We should never engage in the study of the Bible with that self-reliance with which so many enter the domains of science, but with a prayerful dependence upon God and s sincere desire to learn God's will.

Many do not want to belong to God's Church and have many excuses why. We are told "1 Tim 3:15"—that the church is to be the ground and pillar of truth. No church has a right to alter one verse or one word of the Scripture. Those that are proud and feel themselves good enough are hard for Jesus to reach, neither can He use them. Like the Pharisee that stood and prayed thus with himself, "God, I think thee, that I am not as other men are, extortioners, unjust, adulterers, or even as this publican. I fast twice in the week, I give tithes of all that I possess." What does Jesus say about people who think themselves good enough for heaven? Matt 9:12—"They that be whole need not a physician, but they that are sick." If you do not feel good enough to belong to God's church, that is a good sign that God wants you in His church.

Some say they cannot belong to the church because there are to many hypocrites in the church. By the authority of God's Word the church is not a museum where you find perfect people, but rather the church is a hospital where men and women to come together to gain strength. Friends, never imagine yourself to be better off spiritually outside the church than on the inside. A hypocrite is one that knows to do better, but does it not. There are far more hypocrites on the outside of the church than on the inside.

Jesus says-Matt 13:48—"Again the kingdom of heaven is like unto a net, that was cast into the sea, and gathered of every kind." It gathered good and bad fish alike. Christians must be very careful and tolerant with the faults of others. It is easy to be unkindly intolerant. Christians are not to judge others. Matt 7:15—says -"there will be wolves in sheep's clothing that will come in not sparing the flock, but will try to dismember the flock while supposedly they are still in the church.

Christians must cling together, if one chooses to go alone, even though all are not at the same knowledge of their experience, its hard to stand alone, we need each other. Like a fire of many coal's that are flaming hot, when one takes one coal away from the fire, and puts it by itself, soon the flame flickers and dies out, leaving just an ugly black hunk of charcoal. If that hunk of charcoal is returned to the fire, among the other coals, it will again begin to glow and burst into flames. Why? Because it was returned and united with the body pf coals. People are the same, we need each other, Jesus said in Hebrews 10:25—"Not neglecting to meet together, as is the habit of some, but encouraging one another, and all the more as you see the Day drawing near." There is another advantage in belonging to the Church. There is strength in united prayer. Jesus said in Matt 18:19-20—When two of you agree on anything that you shall ask, the Father will hear and answer your prayer. We need to continue to be united with the church body, for having our names severed is like a branch severed from a tree, it will die. Jesus gave reference to such when speaking about the ninety and nine. Would every church member take the attitude and rather than casting stones and trying to scatter, we could through love draw them back to God.

There are those who say, "Yes, I want to be a Christian, but I don't want to belong to a church." This is the same as to come to a minister and say, "I want to live with this man, but I don't want to marry him. Can you fix it up some way so I can live with him without marrying him? Many people are in this way trying to commit spiritual adultery with Christ, wanting to live with Him yet not be a part of Him or His body, the church. This cannot be done ! There is a lot of people who are called Christians who try to act like Christians, try to have the ammunition of Christians, but do not want to unite with the body of Christ. We are not to rest in the idea that because we are members of a Church that we are saved, while we cling to our old habits, with threads of worldly ideas and customs. Pass judgment upon yourself, and by faith claim the cleansing blood of Christ to remove the stains from your character. When Christ appears, it will not be to correct the evils in our lives. This preparation must all be made before Christ comes.

The reward of a relationship with Christ is a comfort. Here are some of the rewards:

> Rom 8:14-15—adoption into the family of God.
> Rom 8: 15-16—free from fear—a child of God.
> Rom 14:17—Personal Peace and happiness
> Rom 15:13—Hope instead of Hopelessness
> John 14:17— The Spirit of Truth dwelling in you.
> John 16:7,13—Superhuman counsel—we will be
> led into all truth.

THE POWER OF THE GOSPEL!

Rom 1:16—I am not ashamed of the Gospel of Christ; for it is the power of God unto salvation to everyone that believeth; to the Jew first, and also to the Greek." Whoever wishes to know how great God's power is, has only to look how God delivered Israel from Egypt. [Ex 15:3-19]. This same power will accompany the preaching of the Gospel in the days just before the coming of the Lord in all the earth.

People today are guilty of false faith as Israel was after the battle of Jericho. Israel thought they had faith to over throw the people and city of Ai, and went of their own to battle against the men of Ai. The men went up against the men of Ai, so the men of Ai smote the men of Israel and the men of Israel fled and the hearts of the people became like water—Joshua 7:2-5. The lesson is "it is better to go where the Lord leads, not what we think ! It was the beginning of apostasy for Israel as they thought how they could defeat Ai on their own strength. The lesson is for us today. We cannot win the battle against evil our selves, we need the power of our God to lead us in the battle of evil. Nothing is to big for our God.

Jesus knows us by the words that we have spoken of Him privately, that we believe His words, but many will not take their stand for Him publicly, for fear they will be ridiculed among their circle of friends.

God had promised to give Israel the land, and it could not be obtained, except as a gift ! The same is the gift of heaven and eternal life for people today. We can only receive the gift of heaven and eternal life as a gift. As the people of Israel tried to work out their own idea of how to take the promised land, there are people today doing the same. Many people want to be the chosen people of God, but like the people that went against Ai, they want to do as they choose, rather than the Ten simple ways of God. Ps 81:13—"Oh that My people had hearkened unto Me, and walked in My ways !" How true is this today? Many today choose their own way with the Lord in how to honor, rather than as God has asked. The people of Israel fought throughout all their national existence. It was not God's purpose that they fight, but their minds were blinded by unbelief.

Two things have always been true—"No person liveth unto themselves and God is no respecter of persons," and these two truths combined form a third, which is that whenever God bestows any gift or advantage upon any person, it is that He may use it for the benefit of others. The gospel is the power of God to salvation." Knowledge of God is not faith ! The devils know that there is one God, but they have no faith. God saves people, not because they are good, but because they are willing to be made good !

Many think of the old Testament as a bunch of rules and think of the New Testament as something without laws and commandments. When the rich young ruler in scripture asked Jesus what he needed to do to inherit eternal life, what did Jesus say? Luke 18:18-20—"You know the commandments." Following Christ is simple, only ten things we are asked to do ! Mankind has tried to expand on God's law and that is the reason for so many different churches today !

Decide to follow Jesus for the rest of your life. We may not have tomorrow. We may be persecuted by family or loved ones, but what is persecution compared with eternity where there is no 'sin' or death? Remember the prophets and our brethren, who were put to death because they dared to be of faith for Christ. If your faith is private, go public with it.

Is your pride keeping you from dependence on God ? You can enter God's Kingdom only through the narrow gate. The road to hell is broad, and its gate are wide, for there are many who choose that way. Matt 7:13-14—"Because narrow is the gate and difficult is the way which leads to life, and there are few who find it." Friend, do you trust someone more that you should, who is in the position of Scriptural authority ? If you are following someone more closely than you are following Christ, then redirect to follow Christ. We are reminded in Matt 7:15-16—"Beware of false prophets who come to you in sheep's clothing, but inwardly they are ravenous wolves. You will know them by their fruits." It is better to get Godly wisdom from the Holy Scriptures than from anyone.

DOES THE GOSPEL INCLUDE THE LAW OF GOD?

The great sin of the Jews was their rejection of Christ. They did not trust in God to supply their needs which was not always best for them. The great sin of the world today is the rejection of the Law of God, the foundation of His government in heaven and earth. Matt 24:35—"heaven and earth will pass away, but My words shall not pass away." It was the love of God to man that prompted Him to express His will in the ten precepts of the Decalogue. The Law sends men to Christ, and Christ points them to His Law. The first four commandments,-"supreme love to God'. and the last six, "love to our neighbor."

We know that the ark of God that Moses built is a copy of the ark of God which is in heaven. Rev 11:19—Tells of the ark in heaven that Moses was to copy. This ark holds the Law of God for all God's creations. All heaven abides by the Law of God and all that go to heaven when Christ comes will have the Law of God engraved upon their heart—Heb 8:10. The law of God will be the standard in the judgment that takes place before Christ comes. Rom 2:12-16—"the doers of the law shall be justified." Proverbs 28:9—"He that turns his ear from hearing the Law, even his prayer shall be abomination." 1 John 2:3-4 "Now by this we know that we know Him, If we keep His commandments. He who says, 'I know Him' and does not keep His commandments, is a liar, and the truth is not in him." A 'belief' that does not lead to obedience is presumption. 1 John says in V-7—"I write no new commandment to you, but an old commandment which you have had from the beginning." We are not to depend on our obedience to the Law of God, but look to Jesus and believe that we are saved through His Grace. Our obedience to His Law reveals our love to Christ. Faith is not our Saviour.

The Gospel includes the Law of God, and by its own righteousness, causing sin to appear sin. Rom 5:13—"for until the law sin was in the world." Therefore the law was also in the world before it was given upon Mt Sinai—for sin is not imputed when there is no Law." How do we know? Gen 26:5 "Abraham obeyed My voice, and kept My charge, My Commandments, My statutes, and My laws." this was long before Sinai and Israel. Are people today any better than Israel of Moses's time? When God came down to the Mountain and gave Moses His Law of Ten Commandments, what did God require of the people then? Read the directions given to Moses for the people in preparation for God to come to the top of the mountain; to meet and give Moses the Ten commandments, the Law of God for heaven and earth. Read the story in Ex 19 & 20. The people were not to touch the mountain. When God came down to the mountain there was thunder and lightnings, the mountain was in smoke. V-18 of Ex 19 says the mountain quaked greatly. —When Christ comes to redeem those who love's Him, the whole earth and the heavens will shake—Isa 25:19; Hag 2:6-7

The only reason for the giving of the Law upon Mt Sinai, was to give man a more vivid sense of its importance, and of the terrible nature of sin which it forbids, and to lead us to trust in God, instead of ourselves

The law of God in the sanctuary in heaven is the great original, of which the precepts inscribed upon the tables of stone by God, given to Moses on Mt Sinai. Jesus said while on earth—Matt 5:18—"Till heaven and earth pass, one jot or one tittle shall in no wise pass from the Law." Ps 119:89; 111:7-8—"All His commandments are sure. They stand fast forever and ever." Rom 2:12-16—"It is necessary that men should keep the Law of God." The law will be the standard of character in the judgment. The apostle Paul declares "As many as have sinned in the law shall be judged by the law in the day when God shall judge the secrets of men by Jesus Christ."

It was to keep the truth ever before the minds of men, that God instituted the Sabbath in Eden; and so long as the fact that He is our Creator continues to be a reason why we should worship Him, so forever the Sabbath will continue as its sign and memorial. Had the Sabbath been kept, men's thought's and affections would have been led to the Creator as the object of reverence and worship, and would never have been an idolater, an atheist, or an infidel. The keeping of the Sabbath is a sign of loyalty to the true God.

Some today believe and some have been taught that the Law of God; His Ten Commandments was given to Moses, for the people of Israel only. We can read of God reminding Moses and Israel before they had ever gotten to Mt Sinai about God's Law. Soon after the people crossed the Red Sea, they were given food from heaven six days each week, but on the sixth day they were to gather enough for the seventh day, because God rests on His Sabbath Day,-Ex 16:23,25-26. When the people went out to gather food on the seventh day, there was none to gather. The Lord said to Moses when the people went out to gather manna, "How long refuse ye to keep My commandments and My laws-Ex 16: 27-30.

For 40 years the people of Israel kept the Sabbath in the wilderness, eating bread from heaven everyday, before they reached Mt Sinai. Why? God wanted people then and people today, to know the blessings of their Creator. He provides for all our needs.

Why do we people today believe that this is written-"recorded"-only for the sake of those who experienced this, and not for people today? Read what "Rom 15:4" says "For whatsoever things were written afore time were written for our learning, that we through patience and comfort of the Scriptures might have hope." God tested the people then, whether they honor His Law or not. If the people then would honor His law, of the Sabbath, then no doubt, they also would keep His whole Law. James 4:17—"Therefore to him that knoweth to do good, and doth it not, to him it is sin." Eek 18:21—"But if the wicked will turn from from all his sins that he hath committed, and keep all My statutes, and do that which is lawful and right, he shall surely live, he shall not die." Jesus calls death as we know death, "sleep." John 11:11-14—Jesus calls death, sleeping. why? Because Jesus says He is the resurrection, and the life. He that believeth in Me, though he were dead, yet shall he live. 1 Cor 15:20—"But now is Christ risen from the dead, and become the first fruits of them that sleep. following Jesus Christ has been so watered down that repentance—true change has often been discarded. In the Bible, forgiveness is never offered without repentance. Grace is underserved, but it's never cheap. Preacher's offer it like something to sweeten up your life. Salvation is much more costly and real than that. Real repentance is true life change. Believing in God and not having it change your life is senseless. Ps 119:73—"Your hands have made me and fashioned me; Give me understanding, that I may learn Your commandments. V77—"For your law is my delight."

Many today have heard that Christians today are not under the Law. That it was made void at the Cross and by faith in God's Grace. Rom 3:31—explains—"Do we then make void the Law of God through faith? Certainly not ! On the contrary, we establish the Law." We read in Rom 6:14-15 "For sin shall not have dominion over you, for you are not under the law but under grace." When Christ died on the cross, He suffered our penalty, for our sins that we may choose to live according to His Law of Love and have a home with Him. We are now under Grace. V-16—"Do you not know that whom you present yourselves slaves to obey, you are that one's slaves whom you obey, whether of sin leading to death, or obedience leading to righteousness." The only way to know what is sin, is by the Law of God.

God can't downgrade the Law or disregard or change it or dispense with it—not even to save the life of His own Son. So don't let anyone ever tell you that Jesus died on the cross to do away with His Law. The commandments that were nailed to the cross were the commandments of the sacrifice's of the lamb's that pointed to when the Son of God would come as the Lamb of God and be sacrifice His life for our sins. This is just the opposite what many hear today from those who should know ! Had the law been able to be changed or over looked, then Jesus didn't need to have died and Calvary was only a meaningless drama. Jesus died on the cross because there was no other way to save you and me. Jesus died in your and my place, for our sins. The Gospel without the Law is inefficient and powerless. The Law and the Gospel are a perfect whole. The Law of God produces love and faith unfeigned.

DID OUR FORE-FATHERS
HONOR GOD'S GOSPEL?

Gen 26:5—"Abraham obeyed My voice, and kept My charge, My commandments, My statutes, and My Laws." Where and when is there recorded in the Gospel that God has changed any part of His Laws?

Paul preached the Gospel—1 Cor 10:16—"for, though I preach the Gospel, I have nothing to glory of; for necessity is laid upon me; woe is unto me, if I preach not the Gospel."

Scripture says that people that believe the Gospel follow the Shepherd. John 10:26,27—"My sheep hear My voice, and I know them, and they follow Me."

In sparing the life of Cain, the son of Adam and Eve, God gave the world an example of what would be the result of permitting the sinner to live and continue a course of sin. Cain's desendents were led into sin, until the wickedness of men was so great, "Every imagination of the thoughts of his heart was only evil continually." "The earth also was corrupt before God, and the earth was filled with violence"-Gen 6:5,11. But Noah found Grace in the eyes of the Lord and the Lord said to Noah, make thee an ark of gopher wood and rooms for every living thing of all flesh to keep alive with thee; Gen 6:1-22. After one hundred and twenty years of building the ark, no one believed Noah or God. God gave mankind "seven days" to choose if they would believe the truth about what was coming upon the earth. Seven days the doors were open for all to come into the ark and be saved. When the door was shut, rain which had never before been seen began to fall. Noah had preached for 120 years of what was to come upon the earth while building the ark, but the people then were like some today, They will never make a choice. They refuse to believe the truth-GOSPEL-in the word of God. For seven days after Noah and his family were in the ark and all the animals with the door open, the people could have come in to be saved, but the choice has to be made by each person today as well as then. God does not use force only Love !

Following Jesus Christ has been so watered down that people think they need not repent of their sins. True repentance and change has often been discarded. Scripture does not suggest that forgiveness is offered without true repentance. Some pastors offer God's Grace like something to sweeten up your life. Real repentance is true life change. Believing in God and not having it change your life is senseless. David says—Ps 119:73—"Your hands have made me and fashioned me, give me understanding." V-77—"for your Law is my delight."

Martin Luther made a solemn vow to study carefully and to preach with fidelity the word of God, not the sayings and doctrines of the popes, all the days of his life. He firmly declared that Christians should receive no other doctrines than those which rest on the authority of the sacred Scriptures. Luther saw the danger of exalting human theories above the word of God. Luther taught that truth and error, there is an irrepressible conflict. To uphold and defend the one is to attack and overthrow the other. Luther clearly showed that the gospel of Christ is the most valuable treasure of the church, and that the Grace of God, therein revealed, is freely bestowed upon all who seek it By repentance and faith. Half-hearted Christians are worse than infidels; for their deceptive words and noncommittal position lead many astray. The infidel shows his colors. The lukewarm Christian deceives both parties. He is neither a good worlding nor a good Christian. Satan uses him to do a work no other one else can do. We are on guard against dishonoring God by professing to be His people, and then going directly contrary to Christ and the Gospel.

Luther wrote: "We cannot attain to the understanding of Scripture either by study or by the intellect. Our first duty is to begin our study with prayer. Entreat the Lord to grant you, of His great mercy, the true understanding of His Word." These truths will stir the enmity of Satan and of man who love the fables that he has devised. Enemies of the Gospel appeal to the customs and traditions of men.

God has never selected as a prophet either the high priest or any other great personage, but ordinarily God chose low and despised men, once even the shepherd Amos. In every age the saints have had to reprove the great, kings, priest, and the wise men, at the peril of their lives. The principles of Truth, were valued above houses and lands, friends, kindred, even life itself.

THE SOURCE OF LIFE, THE GOSPEL

All plant life is the manifestation of the life of the word of the Lord. The life in His word caused corn to grow even today. All the food mankind has is that which comes from the Word of God. No one can see the life in grain, or bread made from it, We experience life ! God supplies life in plants that can be eaten that supplies our bodies with life.

So it was with the children of Israel in the desert for 40 years. The manna was a test of their loyalty to the Law of God. If we allow Christ to dwell in our hearts by faith in His word, not some parts, but the whole—He will bring into our lives the keeping of His whole Law, including the Sabbath.

It is a custom among Christians to return thanks when we eat. The trouble is that giving thanks is so often a form, not from the heart. We have nothing except that which comes from God. God gives food and the most we can do is gather His bounty. We ought not to consider any of our possessions as our own, but to hold them simply in trust for the Lord.

The Gospel is like the manna from God, and like water from the Rock. God is the source of both, for He created them. Jesus Christ is the Rock upon which His church is built, the living Stone, disallowed indeed of men, but chosen of God—1 Peter 2:4. Scripture says we can be living stones when we build upon the word of the Lord—"Gospel". But we can also be a stone of stumbling and a rock of offense, by being disobedient to His Word—1 Peter 2:7-8. We are told in 1 Cor 3:11—"For other foundations can no man lay other than that is laid, which is Jesus Christ. Who ever builds not on Him, builds on the shifting sand." What do we see today, all the different churches with different Gospel's. We are told how this would come about in —Jeremiah 2:12-13 "For My people have committed two evils; they have forsaken Me, the fountain of living water, and hewed out cisterns, that hold no water."

The person who sees and acknowledges God in all his works, and gives thanks, will live a righteous life. Like the gift of water, if we thought of God as the provider of it, as the water of life, our lives would be continually subject to His control, and acknowledging our life that comes from God. As we become the dwelling—place of God, to reproduce Christ again before the world, and living streams flow from us to refresh the faint and weary, heaven will be revealed on this earth.

God designed the Bible to be a lesson book for all mankind, youth, and manhood, and to be studied through time. The study of the scriptures is the means divinely ordained to bring men into closer connection with their Creator and to give them a clearer knowledge of His will.

Jesus died as a sacrifice for man because mankind can do nothing to recommend themselves to God. The merits of a crucified and risen Saviour are the foundation of the christian's faith. 1 John 1:7—"The blood of Jesus Christ, His Son cleanest us from all sin."

WHAT IS THE GOSPEL ABOUT THE COMING OF CHRIST?

C hrist declares that there will exist similar unbelief, concerning His second coming, as the people of Noah's day "Knew not until the flood came, and took them all away," so in the words of our Saviour, "shall also the coming of the Son of man be." Matt 24:39.

How many churches are tended like sick lambs by those who ought to be seeking for lost sheep and all the time millions without the knowledge of Christ are perishing? The wonderful Love of Christ will melt and subdue hearts, when the reiteration of doctrine would accomplish nothing.

Rev 1:1-3—"Blessed is he that hearth, and they that hear the words of this prophecy, and keep those things which are written therein; for the time is at hand."

Though no man knoweth the day or the hour of our Lord's coming, we are instructed and required to know when it is near. To disregard and refuse or neglect to know when Christ coming is near, will be as fatal for us as it was for those who lived in the days of Noah to not know the flood was coming.

We can read that some claim Christ will come secret to those He wants to take home to heaven. Some say Christ will come and raptured secretly those He wants to save. But what does the Gospel teach? 1 Thess 1:7-8 "the Lord Jesus shall be revealed from heaven with His mighty angels, In flaming fire "taking vengeance on them that know not the Gospel of our Lord Jesus Christ." Isa 26:19-21—"Thy dead men shall live,—Awake and sing, ye that dwell in the dust. Ps 50:3-5—"Our God shall come, and shall not keep silence. Ps 96:12—"He will judge the world with righteousness, and the people with "His Truth." 2 Thess 1:7-8—"when the Lord Jesus shall be revealed from heaven with His mighty angels,—taking vengeance on them that know not God, and that obey not the Gospel of our Lord Jesus Christ;" There is a difference between His coming to "Mt Sinai" and His coming to take home to heaven those who obey His Law. At sinai, the mountain quaked greatly—Ex 19:8. At His second advent -Heb 12:26-"The whole heavens shall pass away with a great noise."

When Christ comes back to redeem those that love Him, Christ will call them who sleep in the earth by the same spirit that raised Jesus from the dead—Rom 8:11. What a promise we have in God's Book !

What we hear from the pulpits in our Churches today, is not the "Gospel of God." How do we know? Compare what is taught from the word of God, and you may wonder where and what they have read and studied for their teachings.

The teachings so widely echoed from popular pulpits today, that the second advent of Christ is coming to each individual at death, is a device to divert the minds of men from Christ personal coming in the clouds of heaven to deceive people and believe a lie of Satan. For years Satan has thus been saying, "Behold, He is in the secret chambers" and many souls are lost by accepting this deception.

The New World Dictionary by webster says that the Gospel is —"Good news"—good story—History— the teachings of Jesus and the Apostles—the history of the life and teachings of Jesus—a belief proclaimed or accepted as absolutely Truth."

Friend, have you accepted the Gospel as truth or is the Gospel just a good story? Time is going to end and what will you and I do? Will we live the Gospel that has told us how to live and look forward to the day when Christ comes? Or—will we live as Israel of old, that which we choose rather than the Gospel of God ?

Satan contests every claim put forth by the Son of God and employs men as his agents to fill the life of everyone with suffering and sorrow. Satan exerted all his power to destroy Jesus, for he see's the Savior's mercy and love, His compassion and pitying tenderness, are representing to the world the character of God.

We seldom think of the evil angels who are constantly seeking access to us, and against whose barracks we have, in our own strength, we have no method of defense. If permitted, evil angels can distract our minds, disorder and torment our bodies, destroy our possessions and our lives. We can read this about the life of Job in our Bible's. but those who follow Christ are ever under His watch-care. The wicked one cannot break through the guard which God has stationed about His people.

WHAT IS THE GOSPEL ABOUT DEATH AND OUR SOUL?

1 Cor 15:56—"The sting of death is sin, and the strength of sin is the law." Rom 7:8—"Without the Law, sin is dead." The law sets forth sin in its true character, and with it, the power of death. We all know that all have sinned—Rom 5:12—and sin and death are inseparable, each is part of the other. It is not possible to sin and shut death out. when we sin, death is part of sin !

Times today are no different from when Paul was preaching the Gospel. The Gospel has always been the same. The only Scripture written for Paul's day and time, was the Old Testament. The gospel today is the same as it was in Paul's day. Acts 17:2—"Paul as his manner was,—reasoned with them out of the Scriptures." V-11—"they received the Word with all readiness of mind, and searched the Scriptures daily, whether those things were so." Oh, that we all should do the same today !

The first sermon ever preached was the immortality of the soul by Satan in the garden of God to Eve. This same sermon is preached today by most pastors of world churches and is as readily received by the majority of people as did Eve. Prominent among many churches today is taught that man's natural immortality and his consciousness lives on in death. The newspaper's proclaims in the Obituaries that loved ones are already in heaven before they are in the graves, or the funeral takes place on earth. The Gospel is found in "Ezk 18:20" —"The soul that sins shall die." Satan said then and is proclaiming today that the soul that sins, it shall not die, but lives eternally. All have sinned and there is no immortal sinner on this earth regardless of who teaches that the soul goes to heaven at death. Rev 20:12—"And the dead were judged according to their works, by the things which were written in the books, according to their works." Do people today wonder at the strange infatuation which renders men so credulous concerning the words of Satan and so unbelieving in regard to the words of God ? Many believe they go to heaven or that their soul goes to heaven as soon as their breath stops. But where is this found in Scripture? Satan is the only one who claimed this to Eve in the garden of Eden. But many today like Eve have accepted this same lie. This is why we should know what God says in His Word.

Not only has Satan convinced people of his lie about sin and death, now Satan make's special effort to have people believe another lie. In man's natural immortality as Satan wants people to believe, Satan leads people to believe that the sinner will live in eternal misery. Satan represents God as a revengeful God, declaring that God plunges into hell all those who do not please Him, into eternal flames. Satan clothes his own attributes as the Benefactor of mankind. Cruelty is that of Satan. God is Love, and all that God created as pure, holy and lovely, until sin was brought in by Satan.

The most universal Question which comes to the human heart is "what lies beyond death and the grave ? Let us be sure we understand the meaning of the word immortality, to be mortal means to be subject to death and immortality is not subject to death. The Gospel says that life and immortality came to light through the Gospel. With out the Gospel, we could not possess immortality.

The great majority today believe that we have innate immortality—that we are naturally immortal and cannot die. They say "Oh, our body can die, but not the soul, it is immortal.

But the bible says that we should seek for immortality. If we had it already, we wouldn't need to seek it, would we ?

We as Christians suffer death, we are buried, just the same as those who do not accept the Lord. The Bible says that the life we have, even as Christians is not yet in us, it is in Christ. We read this in — 1 John 5:11—"This is the testimony, that God gave us eternal life, and this life is in His Son." Everywhere that Scripture refers to our possession of this gift of life, it says that we have it now—it's ours now. God says though given to us, it is in His Son. It is not in us yet. "He gave us eternal life, and this life in in His Son. You say this is a contradiction? No, not at all. Its as if I am going to bequeath to my son a sum of money and when I die that money will be his; but the will further stipulates that he doesn't receive possession of it until he is of age. It must stay in trust in the bank until he is of age and then he may possess it.

Now when does that money become his ? Some will say, when the father dies, others say when he's of age. the answer is that the money is his immediately at his father's death. it belongs no one else. But those who say when the son is of age really meant that he can't posses the money until he is of age, he can't possess the money or use it until he is of age but it is the son's and he can only receive possession of the money when he is of the right age. John 3:36—"He who believes in the Son has everlasting life, and he who believes not the Son shall not see life; but the wrath of God abideth in him. When we believe, we have life; Christ gives it to us, but it's kept in the 'life bank' of heaven, we do not posses eternal life till Christ comes, and then we receive the gift of eternal life. All those who love our Lord will receive eternal life when Jesus Christ comes. 1 Cor 15:53—"For this corruptible must put on incorruption, and this mortal must put on immortality." When Christ comes, is when we receive our immortality for V-54 says this. But you say "Where does an individual spend the time between his death and the resurrection day, when he receives this immortality?" Well, in Job 17:13 the Bible says "If I wait, the grave is mine house." We also can read in John 5:28-29—"marvel not at this; for the hour is coming, in which all that are in the graves shall hear His voice, and shall come forth; they that have done good, unto the resurrection of life, and those that have done evil, unto the resurrection of damnation." At the second coming of Christ, at the last trumps—tells when we possess the immortality. Over and over the Scriptures speaks of death as an experience of sleep. The living are not going to precede the dead, to heaven, and the dead are not to precede the living. We're all going to go to heaven with Christ when He comes at the same time.

Hebrews 9:27—"And it is appointed unto men once to die, but after this the judgment." God is judging mankind now. iI man is to be saved, he must love God and his fellowman, for this is what the Gospel says. No one will precede others while they live or at death, but only when Christ comes to redeem those that love Jesus Christ. We may believe what we may think about death, but unless it is from Scripture, it's not true, and we hear a lot today that is not from Scripture.

We have all heard all our lives from preacher's that the soul has gone to heaven, when we die, but we never hear what happens to the soul who does not go to heaven. Well, the "Truth" is that neither the saints nor the sinners soul goes anywhere at death except to the grave. That's what the Bible tells us. The dead sleep in the grave until the resurrection day, when Christ comes to redeem those who Love him.

Satan is seeking to overcome people today, as he overcame our first parents, by shaking our confidence in our Creator. How repulsive to every emotion of love and mercy, and even to our sense of justice, is this doctrine that the wicked dead are tormented with fire and brimstone in an eternally burning hell fire. Yet this doctrine has been widely taught and is still embedded in many of the creeds of Christendom. The appalling views of God which spread over the world from the teachings from the pulpit have made thousands, yes millions of skeptics and infidels. When we turn from the testimony of God's word, and accept false doctrines because our fathers taught them, we fall under the condemnation pronounced upon Babylon; we are drinking of the wine of her abomination.

This doctrine that the wicked dead are tormented with fire and brimstone in an eternally burning hell fire is revolting and has driven people to the opposite error. they believe that finally they will be received into God's favor, presuming upon God's mercy. Those who flatter themselves that God is too merciful to execute justice upon the sinner, have only to look to the cross of Calvary. The death of the spotless Son of God testifies that the wages of sin is death. Christ the sinless became sin for mankind. Christ bore the guilt of our transgressions, until His heart was broken and His life crushed out. All this sacrifice was made that sinners might be redeemed. This is the "Gospel" today and will be forever.

Many people today believe that when they die, they pass directly to heaven at the hour of death, if this were so, we might well covet death rather than life. Ezekiel 18:4—"all souls are mine; the soul of the father, so also the soul of the son is mine; the soul that sins, it shall die." Matt 10:28—And fear not them which kill the body, but are not able to kill the soul; but rather fear Him which is able to destroy both soul and body in Hell."

Many people today have heard and believe that when they die that their soul goes directly to heaven. We all have heard this from people who should know better. Many who teach this, base their hope on [[Gen 35:18]—"And it came to pass, as her soul was in departing [for she died] that she called his name Benoni ; but his father called him Benjamin." And —Micah 6:7—"shall I give my firstborn for my transgression, the fruit of my body for the sin of my soul?" And Ps 121:7—"The Lord shall preserve thee from all evil; He shall preserve thy soul." and Ps 23:3—"He restores my soul." All the different text in Scripture helps us to understand that when the Lord created Adam and Eve, God breathed into them the breath of life and they became a living soul. When man dies, the breath returns to God. What about the soul? We don't know because we are not told. what we may think is not part of the Gospel! We know that when Christ comes for those who love and obey His Law of Love, we will be raised from the grave and with those who are alive, will go home to heaven with Christ. God will restore those who He takes to heaven with the breath of life, and soul, to live with Him for eternity. The wicked who put Christ to death will be raised to see Jesus come, then will be destroyed by the brightness of His coming. The Lord bears long with those who choose to believe not the gospel of Truth. The gospel when accepted leads to eternal life. The destiny of the wicked and those who refuse to believe the Gospel, choose their own destiny, and God is just and merciful.

There is a tombstone in Brunswick in the state of Maine that bears a birthdate and two death dates. It reads; born June 10, 1794;— Died Nov 10:1848—Fell asleep May 9, 1882.—

Infant, Coob was baptized on Nov 10; 1848, and he asked that the date of his conversion be carved on his tombstone after he was laid to rest in the grave on May 9, 1882, at the age of 88. This was the way he wanted to share his faith even after he died. His tombstone includes text from the Holy Bible, "Remember the Sabbath Day to keep it Holy. Cobb's unique witness from the grave has touched the hearts of many people, including church members. He knew he needed to die to self and then he could become alive when Jesus Christ comes for those who love Him and honor the Gospel of God.

Paul of Scripture says in Acts 24:15—"All alike go down into the grave, and there shall be a resurrection of the dead, both of the just and the unjust." John says in John 5:28—"for the hour is coming, in which all that are in the graves shall hear His voice." Hosea 13:14—"I will ransom them from the power of the grave, I will redeem them from death. O death, I will be your plagues! O grave, I will be your destruction" !

Since it is impossible for God, consistency with His justice and mercy to save the sinner in his sins, God deprives him of the existence which his transgressions have forfeited and of which ha has proved himself unworthy. Thus will be made an end of sin, with all the woe and ruin which have resulted from it.

Is taught by some that the soul is natural immortal and rest the doctrine of consciousness in death, like eternal torment, which is opposed to the Gospel in Scripture. According to this popular belief, the redeemed in heaven are acquainted with all that takes place on the earth and especially with the lives of the friends and family, whom they left behind. How can this be a source of happiness to those who die, to know the troubles of the living, tp witness the sins committed by their own loved ones, and the sorrows, disappointments of those facing each day ? How revolting is the belief that as soon as the breath leaves the body, the soul of the impenitent is consigned to the flames of hell ! To what depths of anguish must those be who see their friends passing to the grave unprepared, to enter upon an eternity of woe and sin ! Many have been driven to insanity by this borrowing thought. What does the Scripture say—Acts 24:15—"there shall be a resurrection of the dead, both of the just and the unjust." I believe God's Holy Word is enough for our trust, His Word is true ! 1 Cor 24:15—"For as in Adam all die, even so in Christ shall all be made alive." John 5:28—"For the hour is coming, in which all that are in the graves shall hear His voice." —V-29—"And shall come forth; they that have done good to the resurrection of life; and they that have done evil, unto the resurrection of damnation." We read in 'Obadiah 15-16—"the day of the Lord is near all the heathen; —they shall be as they had not been." Oh, to know the gospel Truth ! David says—Ps 146:3-4—"Put not your trust in princes, nor in the son of man, in whom there is no help. His breath goeth forth, he returns to his earth; in that very day his thoughts perish." Solomon bears the same Gospel—Eccl 9:5,6,10—"The living know that they shall die, but the dead know not anything. Their love, and their hatred, and their envy is now perished; neither have they any more a portion forever in anything that is done under the sun. There is no work, nor device, nor knowledge, nor wisdom, in the grave whether thou goest."

Some today think of the words of Jesus while on the cross to the thief who ask Jesus to remember him when He comes. The thief didn't ask to go to heaven that day. He said "Lord, remember me when Thou comest into thy kingdom. And Jesus said to him, "Verily I say unto thee today, Thou shalt be with Me in Paradise"—Luke 23:42-43. According to Scripture, the thief didn't die that day. Scripture says that they broke the legs of the two thieves who were crucified with Christ, because they were still alive when taken off the cross. But when they came to Jesus Christ, they were surprised to see that He appeared dead already. One of the soldiers thrust a spear into Christ side, to make sure He was dead, and water and blood gushed out. So we know that the thief wasn't dead when the day was ended, but Jesus had died.

Did Jesus or the thief go to heaven that day? No, because On Sunday, the first day of the week, Mary came to the tomb and Jesus said to her, "don't hold [touch] Me for I have not ascended to the Father yet, but go to My breathen and say to them, I am ascending to My Father and your Father." John 20:17.

The thief knew then, that Jesus was the Saviour of mankind

and would one day come to redeem those that love and obey His Gospel.

Oh that Christians today would study Scripture and know the gospel Truth ! Ps 6:5 and Ps 115:17—"In death there is no remembrance of Thee; In the grave who shall give Thee thanks? The dead praise not the Lord, neither any that go down into silence." Acts 2:29—"of the patriarch David, that he is both dead and buried, and his sepulcher is with us unto this day." V-34— "For David is not ascended into the heavens."

We seldom hear the Gospel about death in the present day. there is not a doctrine in the present system of preaching which is treated with more neglect. Our judgment does not take place at death. Paul—Acts 17:31—"Because He hath appointed a day, in which He will judge the world in righteousness, by that Man whom He hath ordained; whereof He hath given assurance unto all men, in that He hath raised Him from the dead." We also read in —Jude 6—"The angels which kept not their first estate, but left their own habitation, He hath reserved in everlasting chains under darkness unto the judgment of that great day." Jude 14-15—"Behold, the Lord cometh with ten thousands of His saints, to execute judgment upon all." John says in —Rev 20:12— "I saw the dead, small and great, stand before God; the books were opened—the dead were judged out of those things which were written in the books, according to their works."

But as some believe today, that at death, we are taken to heaven or writhing in the flames of hell, what need of a future judgment ? The Gospel teachings of God's Word on these important points are neither obscure nor contradictory; that they may be misunderstood by common people. Will the wicked be summoned from the place of torment to receive sentence from the Judge of all the earth when Christ comes ?

No where in Scripture is found the statement that the righteous go to their reward or the wicked to their punishment at death. 1 Thess 4:14—Job 14:10-12—Eccl 12:6—"In that very day when the silver cord is loosed—man's thoughts perish."

Ps 78:50—"He did not spare their soul from death." —Ps 115:17—"The dead do not praise the Lord, nor do any who go down to silence."

Ezekiel 18:4—"Behold, all souls are Mine; The soul of the father as well as the soul of the son is Mine; The soul that sins shall die."

Eccl 3:19-20—"for what happens to the sons of men also happens to animals; one thing befalls them; as one dies, so does the other. They all have one breath, man has no advantage over the animals, for all is vanity. All go to one place; all are from dust, and all return to dust."

Eccl 9:5—"The living know that they will die; but the dead know nothing.

1 Thess 4:15—"we who are alive and remain until the coming of the Lord will by no means precede those who are asleep in the graves."

Rev 1:5—"Jesus Christ is the first born from the dead."

The gospel is the same today and never will be changed. — Mal 3:6—"For I am the Lord, I change not; therefore ye sons of Jacob are not consumed." Except those who are kept by the power of God, through faith in His word, the whole world will be swept into the ranks of Satan's delusion of the dead. God does not force the will or judgment of any person. God takes no pleasure in a slavish obedience. He desires that the creatures of His hands shall love Him because He is worthy of Love. He would have them obey Him because they have an intelligent appreciation of His wisdom, justice, and benevolence. And all who have a just conception of these qualities will love Him because they are drawn toward Him in admiration of His attributes.

We read in Rev 14 about "Babylon" a form of false or apostate religion. This unfaithful apostate church religion allows the love of worldly things to occupy the mind and soul, and is likened to the violation of the marriage vow.

There could not be any hope for mankind, had not God, by the sacrifice of His Son brought immortality within reach for mankind. Death has passed upon all mankind, because all have sinned. Christ hath brought life and immortality to light through the Gospel. Rom 5:12 & 2 Tim 1:10.

The only one who promised Adam life in disobedience was the great deceiver. Satan said—"you shall not surely die." This is the first sermon ever preached upon the immortality of the soul. many people believe this lie today ! We read and hear from pulpits today that loved ones are in heaven before their funeral is over and laid to rest in the earth. Satan is still at his deceiving ways to turn away people from the gospel.

Those who have chosen Satan as their leader and have been controlled by his power are not prepared to enter the presence of God. Pride, deception, have become fixed in their characters. Can they enter heaven to dwell forever with those they despised and hated on earth ? Truth will never be agreeable to a liar; meekness will not satisfy self—esteem and pride; purity is not acceptable to the corrupt; disinterested love does not appear attractive to the selfish. what source of enjoyment could heaven offer to those who are wholly absorbed in earthly and selfish interests ? Could those whose heart's are filled with hatred for truth and holiness mingle with the heavenly throng and join their songs of Praise to the Lord?

Thousands reject the Word of God as unworthy of belief and with eager confidence receive the deceptions of Satan. Skeptics and scoffers denounce the bigotry of those who contend for the faith of prophets and apostles, and they divert themselves by holding up to ridicule the solemn declarations of the Scriptures concerning Christ and the plan of salvation, and the retribution to be visited upon the rejecters of the truth. Except those who are kept by the power of God, through faith in His word, the ranks of this delusion, people are fast being lulled to s false security, to be awakened only by the outpouring of the wrath of God.

There is not a doctrine in the Gospel on which more stress is laid; and there is not a doctrine in the present system of preaching which is treated with more neglect than when we die. No where in Sacred Scripture is found the statement that the righteous go to their reward or the wicked to their punishment at death. The Bible clearly teaches that the dead do not go immediately to heaven. They are represented as sleeping until the resurrection. ! Thessalonians 4:14; & Job 14:10-12. all the dead will be awakened by the trump of God when He comes with all the angels. What a wonderful time this will be for all that look for our Lord's coming !

THE GOSPEL OF RIGHTEOUSNESS

Rom 3:22-23—"Even the Righteousness of God, which is by Faith in Jesus Christ unto all and upon all them that believe, for there is no difference; for all have sinned, and come short of the glory of God." The Lord declares by the prophet Isaiah; "I, even I, am He that blotteth out the transgressions for Mine own sake, and will not remember thy sins." Jesus Christ is our Judge, He knows each person by name. Christ knows our most secret motives, all have their weight in deciding our destiny. God knows what we have done with the light and truth given us, to make men wise unto salvation. No value is attached to a mere profession of faith in Christ; only the love which is shown by works is counted genuine. It is love alone which in the sight of Heaven makes any act of value. What ever is done from love, however small it may appear in the estimation of men is accepted and rewarded of God. We are not saved in groups. The purity and devotion of one will not offset the want of these qualities in another. We all need to be covered by the righteousness of Christ and this is possible when we love God and our fellow men. God desires men to be happy, and for this reason He gave him the precepts of His Law, that in obeying these, he might have joy at home and abroad. Love to God and love to our neighbor constitute the whole duty of man.

The accounting of faith is done by God, who cannot lie. Rom 10:10—"for with the heart man believes unto righteousness; and with the mouth confession is made unto salvation," Righteousness, which is the fruit of faith, is obedience to the Law of God.

Obedience carries a blessing with it, for it is written V-9—"Blessed are they that do His commandments."

Many believe today that Christ at the cross released us from the Law of God, but Christ death released us from the curse of the Law, which is eternal death because all have sinned. Christ death on the cross, is that we are no longer condemned to eternal death. Christ took our sins we have committed, suffered and died for our sins, that we can have eternal life with Him. If only we all could understand the Gospel of Ps 19:7—"The Law is perfect, converting the soul." The Gospel is revealed in the Law of God. When the Holy Bible is read, the mercy and Love of God will be revealed. It will be seen that God lays upon men none of those heavy burdens. All God asks is a broken and contrite heart, a humble, obedient spirit. By persistent rejection of the Spirit's influence, men cut themselves off from God.

"Both Grace and Truth come by Jesus Christ"—John 1:17. When we believe the words of Christ, the Law is not merely "the voice of words, but a fountain of life." Look at the words of God spoken to Israel at Mt Sinai, which Abraham honored and all mankind is to honor today and will for eternity.

.1. Thou shall have no other gods before Me.
.2. Thou shall not make unto thee any graven image—for I am the Lord thy God am a jealous God.—— showing mercy unto thousands of them that love Me and keep My commandments.
.3. Thou shalt not take the name of the Lord thy God in vain.
.4. Remember the Sabbath day, to keep it Holy—The Lord blessed the Sabbath Day.
.5. Honor thy father and thy mother.
.6. Thou shall not kill.
.7. Thou shall not commit adultery.

.8. Thou shall not steal.

.9. Thou shall not bear false witness.

.10. Thou shall not covet thy neighbor's house.

All these words were spoken by God amid the terrors of Mt Sinai, by 'Him' whose life would be given to us on the cross of Calvery, that our sins could be forgiven. Death is the curse of the Law, which all have sinned, but Christ made possible forgiveness of our sins when He came and died in our place that we could have the choice of forgiveness when we surrender our life to obedience of His Law.

Jesus told the people while on earth, in the sermon on the Mount—Matt 5:17-19. "Think not that I am come to destroy the Law, or the prophets; I am come not to destroy, but to fulfill. For verily I say unto you, Till heaven and earth pass, one jot or one title shall in no wise pass from the Law, till all be fulfilled. Whosoever therefore shall break one of these least commandments, and shall teach men so, he shall be called the least in the kingdom of heaven; but whosoever shall do and teach them shall be called great in the kingdom of heaven." From the very beginning of the controversy in heaven it has been Satan's purpose to overthrow the Law of God and he continues the same upon earth today. Whether this be accomplished by casting aside the Law altogether, or by rejecting one of the precepts, the result will be ultimately the same. He that offends "in one point" manifests contempt for the whole law, his influence and example are on the side of transgression, he becomes "guilty of all"—James 2:10. When we reject the law of God, we reject it's Author.

The life proceeding from Christ at Sinai, as at Calvary, shows that the Gospel is none other than that of the Ten Commandments of God. Not one jot nor one tittle could pass away.—Matt 5:18.

No matter who we are, how we have been taught to believe

about Christ, by our family, relatives, or the Christians of different churches in the world. Jesus Christ has made a promise, —John 6:37—"Him that cometh to Me, I will in no wise cast out." the Lord made another promise—Heb 8:10-12—"I will put My Laws into their mind, and write them on their heart; I will be their God, and they shall be My people, and they shall not teach every man his neighbor, and every man his brother, saying, Know the Lord; for all shall know Me. from the least to the greatest. For I will be merciful to their unrighteousness, and their sins and iniquities will I remember no more." Eph 2:8—"For by Grace are ye saved through faith; and that not of yourselves, it is the gift of God." The Gospel is the "Power of God unto salvation to everyone that believeth."—Rom 1:16. It is when people are ignorant of God's righteousness, that they go about to establish their own righteousness, and refuse to submit themselves to the righteousness of God. To trust in men's way of being righteous is to make a covenant with death. man's covenant with man is worthless. We see these men make covenants the world over. God help people to know the difference, and accept the covenant of our Lord. Many have a zeal for God, but not according to the knowledge of God. the Jewish rulers when Christ walked this earth flattered their pride by sanctioning their cherished opinions and traditions. They were not acquainted with God, and to them His voice was that of a stranger. Does our world hear the same today ?

God meets people just where we are " 2 Cor 4:3-4—"But even if the Gospel is veiled, it is veiled to them that are perishing. Whose minds —the god of this world has blinded them who did not believe." All the false idea's of mankind about salvation comes from the same angel that began his work of seeking to break down the righteous restraints of the Law of God in heaven. When we begin to rationalize the commands of God, where do we stop? How do you know where to quit. if you start to make substitutes ?

In the beginning the Bible tells us a story about Cain and Able. Cain was a brilliant young man, a man who knew how to think. He said, "Here Lord, You said we should bring an offering, a lamb, shed the blood of a lamb and make a sacrifice in order to have our sins forgiven. Now, that is all right for Able, he raises sheep. But I grow the fruit of the ground and my fruit is worth as much as a sacrifice as his sheep. And what is more, I have among the fruit some kinds that can surely symbolize the blood. There is red juice in some of the fruits on the trees as well as some in the ground. I can squeeze some of the juice out and let that symbolize the blood. Sounded good, so why not ? So Cain brought a sacrifice to the Lord contrary to the Lord's command. And the Bible says, God has respect to Able's sacrifice of the lamb's blood, but He rejected Cain's substitute. Cain became so angry over his offering, that he killed his brother adding murder to his sin of disobedience.

It is so easy to rationalize, but to ignore what God says makes us as guilty as Cain. When God says something, He means it.

An old Indian chief came to the mission station and asked for a Bible. Several months later he came back and asked to be baptized. The missionary was happy to oblige and went to get his silver cup of water. The Indian took one look at it and said "To small" ! Then the missionary said, "No you don't have to get in." But the Indian had his Bible to long. He said "If that is the right way to be baptize—you gave me the wrong book ! Friend, we are not to change what God has said.

It is a serious thing to think how far man can depart from the Word of God. Where do we stop? If we call something baptism when it is not, it loses it's meaning.

THE GOSPEL IS
PROMISE'S OF GOD

People today, even professed Christians are sometimes blind. All should be rejoicing in faith every-time we see a rainbow, which is a promise of God. The rainbow is a constant reminder that is from God, that the world will never be destroyed again by a flood. It is a constant witness to all people, but many do not know this.

Those who believe and obey the Gospel of Christ have a promise in 2 Tim 1:10—"Our Saviour, Jesus Christ who hath abolished death, and brought life and immortality to light through the Gospel." People speak of the -Gospel age- and the Gospel dispensation as though the Gospel were an after thought on the part of God, or that which was long delayed for mankind. The Scripture teaches us that "the dispensation" or Gospel age is from lost Eden to Eden restored.

Those who know the Law of God only as it is in the "Bible" and who think that it rests wholly on them to do it, it is a law of works, and as such it does nothing but pronounce a curse upon them. But to those who know the Law of the Lord, it is a law of faith, which proclaims blessings of pardon and peace.

God is long suffering, not willing that any should perish, but come to repentance, and so in harmony as with Abraham, God gave the system of sacrifices and offerings, which could not save them any more than the broken law of works. The very offering of a sacrifice indicated that death is the wages of sin. Everyone can see that the life of a lamb, or bullock was not worth as much as a man's life. Even a human sacrifice could not atone for a single sin. The very offering of a sacrifice indicated that death is the wages and fruit of sin. To the thoughtful person, the law of sacrifice brought conviction of sin, whose only power is death. No one obtained righteousness by the sacrifice of a lamb, but the faith which prompted the offering made man mindful of sin and the penalty of sin. When people today deny the Truth in the Gospel, we are told—2 Thess 2:11-12—"God will send strong delusions, that they believe the lie, they all may be condemned who did not believe the Truth."

In the highest rank of the enemies of the Gospel of Christ, are they who openly and explicitly judge the Law itself, and speak evil of the Law, who teach men to break 'not one only, whether of the least or of the greatest, but all the commandments."—said John Wesley. All who exalt their own opinions above divine revelation, all who change the plain meaning of Scripture to suit their own convenience, or for the sake of conforming to the world are taking upon themselves a fearful responsibility. The written Word of God will measure the character of every person and condemn all whom this unerring test shall declare wanting.

THE GOSPEL OF THE
TRUE SACRIFICE

God gave to us, and made a true sacrifice, which is the sacrifice of His Son, Jesus Christ. What can man do to be worthy of such a gift? Ps 4:5—"Offer the sacrifice of righteousness and put our trust in our Lord." Ps 51:19—"Then shalt Thou be pleased with the sacrifice of righteousness." From the days of Able until now, there has been but one way of life and salvation; only one way of approaching God; only one name under heaven by which people can be saved. There has been no more change in the plan of salvation, nor the requirements for salvation. There is no certain number of people that salvation is offered. All are chosen to be saved, but the choice is left to each person.

When mankind gets the idea that their work's must save them, or that they themselves must do God's work, they cannot be content with attempting to do more than God's commandments. So they teach for doctrine "the commandments of men." adding to them continually until no man could ever enumerate the good works they required, much less do them. Too often religious leaders who are thus praised and reverenced lose sight of their dependence upon God and are led to trust in themselves. As a result they seek to control the minds and consciences of the people, who are disposed to look to them for guidance, instead of looking to the Word of God. The Law of God, His commandments of love are simple enough that every person is able to honor them, not one of them is impossible. Our heavenly Teacher passed by the great men on the earth, the titled and wealthy who were accustomed to receive praise and homage as leaders of the people. They were so proud and self-confident in their boasted superiority that they could not be molded to sympathize with their fellow men and to become co-labors with the humble Man of Nazareth. To the unlearned, toiling fishermen of Galilee was the call addressed; "Follow Me, and I will make you fishers of men."-Matt 4:19. It is God's plan to employ humble instruments to accomplish great results. Then the glory will not be given to men, but to Him who works through them.

The more we search the Scriptures, the clearer appears the contrast between God's Truth and the heresies being taught by men. The word of God is the only infallible authority and the death of Christ is the only complete sacrifice for mankind sins. The gift of salvation belongs to God, and the duty of mankind is obedience to God's Law of Love. It is the cross of Christ alone that open's the gates of heaven, and shuts the gates of hell.

We cannot know how much we owe to God for the peace and protection which we enjoy. It is the restraining power of God that prevents mankind from the power of Satan. But when mankind passes the limits of divine forbearance, that restraint is removed. God leaves the rejectors to themselves, to reap that which they have sown. Every transgression of the Law of God, is a seed sown which yields its unfailing harvest.

THE GOSPEL OF FAITH

KNOWLEDGE OF GOD
IS NOT FAITH !

The demons know that there is one God, but they have no faith. God saves people, not because they are good, but because they are willing to be made good. Faith lifts one out of sinful surroundings and sets us in the way of knowledge. We may profess what we will, but unless our life corresponds with our profession, our faith is dead. Words and acts plainly testify what is in our heart. Remember the heathen woman, the harlot of Jericho, who could utter a lie with a composed countenance, and with no consciousness of guilt. God acknowledged her as one of His people, "Because" she did not turn away from the light of Truth. Her faith lifted her out of her sinful surroundings. No stronger evidence can be found that Christ is not ashamed to have anyone, and to have a harlot recorded in the roll of His ancestry. "The Lord is not willing that anyone should perish, but all come to repentance" -2 Peter 3:9. Conformity to worldly customs converts a person and the church to the world. it never converts the world to Christ. Our faith must be firmly founded upon the Word of God, so when we are asked for our faith, we may be able to give a reason with meekness and fear from the Word of God. It is no easy matter to gain the priceless treasure of eternal life. No one can do this and drift with the current of the world. Blessings come from God on the basis of faith, not Law. The Law of God declares men guilty and imprisons them; Faith sets men free to enjoy liberty in Christ. But liberty is not license to sin.

Many have confused ideas as to what constitutes faith, and they live altogether below their privileges. They confuse feelings with faith, and are continually distressed and perplexed in mind; for Satan takes all possible advantage of their ignorance and inexperience. We must believe that we are chosen of God, to be saved by the exercise of faith, through the Grace of Christ and the work of the Holy Spirit; and we are to praise and glorify God for such a marvelous manifestation of His unmerited favor. David was pardoned of his transgressions because he humbled his heart before God in repentance and contrition of soul, and believed that God's promise to forgive would be fulfilled. David confessed his sin, repented, and was reconverted.

Rom 12:3—"God has dealt to each one a measure of 'faith'. Bellieving and trusting in what we don't see is 'Faith', when based upon the Gospel. Rom 10:17—"So then faith comes by hearing, and hearing by the Word of God." The guard that held Paul and Silas in the Roman jail asked Paul—Acts 16:31—"What must I do to be saved?" Paul said to the man "Believe on the Lord Jesus Christ, and you will be saved, you and your household."

When one rejects the Gospel when proclaimed in its fulness, that is with the mighty power of God, there is nothing more that can be done for people, for there is no greater power than that of God.

If a person says its not necessary for God's people to be separate from the world, he would really be saying that it is not necessary to have the presence of God in our life. We see much of this before our eyes today. Many people today have forsaken our Creator God in their life. We see the result of such. Many want to be known as Christians and yet believe what they like about the Gospel. this is as much a contradiction of the term as saying "Christian Heathen" or a "Christian Sinner." Some are today like Israel of Old, ! Sam 8:20—"We will also be like all the heathen."

Matthew 25—Records about the ten virgins that were waiting for the Bridegroom. All thought they were ready, but some were not allowed to come into the wedding. This is common today, many believe they are Christians, but when the Bridegroom comes, Scripture says Matt 7:21—"but he who does the will of My Father." Oh, that some people could see the path they are following leads not to Christ's Gospel, but to the Adversary's way. A profession of religion has become popular with the world. But religious faith appears so confused and discordant that people know not what to believe as Truth. The sin of the world's impenitence lies at the door of our churches. Many today want to be identified with a Church, and this is no different of what is recorded in -Isa 4:1—"And in that day seven women— "Churches" —will take hold of one man saying, We will eat our own food and wear our own apparel; Only let us be called by your name, to take away our reproach." Do we see the same today in all the different churches in the world?

The Bible declares that before the coming of our Lord, Satan will work with all power and signs and lying wonders, and with all deceiveableness of unrighteousness; and they that received not the love of the Truth, that they might be saved, "Will be left to receive 'strong delusion', that they should believe a lie."—2 Thessalonians 2:9-11.

No man has proved to be a true Christian because he is found in company with the children of God, even in the house of worship and around the table of the Lord. In all the history of the church no reformation has been carried forward without encountering serious obstacles. If a man judges himself by the word of God and finds a perfect harmony through the whole Word, then he must believe he has the Truth. But if he finds the spirit by which he is led does not harmonize with the Law of God-Gospel,- then let him walk carefully, lest he be caught in the snare of the devil. We may profess what we will, but unless our life corresponds with our profession, our faith is dead. Words and acts testify plainly what is in our heart.

We all need to be aware of our self-confidence. Just before Peter's fall, Christ said to Peter, "Simon, behold, Satan hath desired desired to have you, that he may sift you as wheat."-Luke 22:31. But the warning was resented. Peter declared confidently that he would never do what Christ had warned him against. His self-confidence proved his ruin. He tempted Satan to tempt him, and he fell under the arts of the wily foe. Those who trust in self are easily defeated. let us remember that if we do not heed the cautions that God gives us, a fall is before us. We can only be safe as we stand with Jesus who met the tempter with the words—"It is written." We can stand securely in the protection of a "Thus saith the Lord."

WHAT IS THE GOSPEL
IN GOD'S CHURCH?

The last conflict between truth and error is but the final struggle, concerning the Law of God. A battle between the laws of men and the law of God, between the religion of the Bible and the religion of tradition. As Christ was hated without cause, so will His people be hated because they are obedient to the Law of heaven, God's Ten commandments. Beware ! He who dared to force and tempt, and taunt our Lord while He was on earth, had power to take Jesus in his arms and carry Him to the pinnacle of the temple, and up to an exceeding high mountain, will exercise his power to a wonderful degree upon this world. Satan will come personating Jesus Christ and people will fall down and worship this being, whom this world will glorify as Christ. All those whose faith is not firmly established upon the Word of God will be deceived and overcome.

When this takes place, before Christ comes, those who keep the commandments of God and the faith of Jesus, will feel the ire of Satan.

The Law of God, the sacrifice of Jesus Christ on the cross for the sins of mankind is the "Gospel". What we do with this knowledge will determine our life now and forever. What if God wasn't the same all the time? How would we know when He changes? We need not be concerned about changes by God or Jesus Christ for we can read Hebrews 13:8—"Jesus Christ is the same yesterday, today, and forever." Do you believe our Creator

God would create this world and not have a law for the weak beings of His creation?

The word -"CHURCH" is commonly used, but few of those who use it realize that it is from a Greek word which means -"called out". There is but one Church, for the Church is Christ body— Eph 4:4-6—"there is one body and one Spirit —one Lord, one Faith, one baptism, one God and Father of all—." That one Church is composed of those who hear and follow the voice of Christ, for Christ says -John 10:27—"My sheep hear My voice, and they follow Me." When Christ shall have renewed this earth and restored all things as in the beginning, and there is but one fold and one Shepherd, one King in all the earth as it is in heaven. That will be a perfect world. The will of God will be done in all the earth as it is in heaven. Now is the time of preparation. Those who will be gathered, constitute the Church of our Creator. The church is the Kingdom in which God rules alone, and all its power is His power, His only Law is God's Law of Love, His Ten Commandments !

There is no earthly kingdoms that can serve as a model of God's Kingdom. The kingdom of God is not a kingdom of don'ts or do not's depending on human governments, but will be a kingdom of "Love" and unity and harmony that will astonish all. People of this world have tried to change God's Gospel in order to be accepted by more people and yet claim to be His Church proclaiming the Gospel of God. How many churches proclaim to have the Gospel of God? If only Christians would read themselves the Holy Bible and study for themselves, they could know the Gospel of Truth !

Eccl 3:14—"I know that whatever God does, It shall last forever, nothing can be added to it, and nothing taken from it, God does it, that men should fear before Him". Oh that ministers of the Gospel would read this verse of Scripture and understand that one day they will stand before God ! People today are alleging themselves, either following the gospel of God or going their own way which leads to eternal death. Proverbs 16:25—"There is a way that seems right to a man, but the end is the way of death." We cannot depend on anyone on this earth for survival, we can only depend on the One who created this world and mankind.

No one will be without excuse when Christ comes to take His people home. All, have seen since the creation of the world, God's invisible attributes of the things that are made, even His eternal power, so that all will be without excuse, because, although all know God, they did not honor Him, nor was thankful, but became futile in their thoughts, and their foolish hearts were darkened—Rom 1:20—26.

The Gospel of God is simple enough for all to understand. God's Gospel was simple enough for Israel, when they marched around Jericho. If they had not obeyed God and shouted, but only looked at the walls of Jericho, do you think the wall of the city would have fallen? God told the people a simple thing to do, and trust Him. Men have made a mockery of the Gospel of God. Man has tried to change God's seventh—day Sabbath to the first day of creation week and claim it's ok to eat what God says we are not to eat, because it is unclean. Who do you trust, God or man ?

Satan and people have tried to explain that God has changed since Christ death on the cross, but how do we know that to be a lie? Heb 13:8—"Jesus Christ is the same yesterday, today, and forever." We are told in James 1:22—"But be doers of the word, and not hearers only, deceiving yourselves." Ecclesiastes 3:14—"I know that whatever God does, it shall be forever. Nothing can be added to it. And nothing taken from it. God does it, that men should fear before Him."

The gospel is the same in the Old Testament as in the New Testament, for God does not change. The Old Testament foretells the coming of Jesus Christ, and the reason for His coming. The

New Testament tells what Jesus Christ taught and the sacrifice He made, the suffering that He endured for each person that has ever been born on this earth. "The Lord is not slack concerning His promise, as some men count slackness, but is long suffering to us, not willing that any should perish, but that all should come to repentance."—2 Peter 3:9.

Heb 4:2—"for unto us the Gospel was preached, as well as unto them, but the Word preached did not profit them, not being mixed with faith in them that heard it." V-4, "God did rest the seventh day from all His works." The Lord said to David V-7—"Today, if ye will hear His voice, harden not your hearts." V-8 "for if Joshua had given them rest, then He would not afterward have spoken of another day" ? V-10 "for he who has entered His rest has himself also ceased from his works as God did for His." V-11—"Let us labour therefore to enter into that rest, lest any man fall after the same example of unbelief."

"It is impossible for God to lie."-Heb 6:18. We are not forgotten because we may not understand the Truth of the Gospel when we read for our selves what God requires of His people. God will take with Him when He comes; home to heaven to live with Him, and all those that obey His Gospel. 2 Peter 3:9—"The Lord is not slack concerning His promise—but is long suffering toward us, not willing that any should perish, but all should come to repentance." Rom 3:3—"The unbelief of man cannot make the promise of God of none effect."

The day for all to decide to accept God's Gospel is "today". We may not have another day or year, or month next week or even tomorrow, but today only ! The Gospel of God today is the very same Gospel that was preached in the days of Israel and the days that Jesus walked this earth.-Heb 4:2.

God's rest that God created in creation week, after He had created all things, He rested the seventh-day. God wants the same for all His creation. God's work was perfect as God Himself. After God created all the things that He created, His crowning act of creation was creating mankind in His own image, according to His likeness. Gen 2:1-2—"God rested from all His work which He had made." V-3—"God blessed the seventh day and sanctified it." The only day that God blessed and sanctified and He called it the Sabbath-day.

God has given mankind the history of the heavens and this earth, when and how they were created, and by Whom. What was the Gospel for Adam and Eve ? Gen 2:8—"The Lord planted a garden eastward in Eden and there He put man whom He had created." Gen 3—Tells that God told Adam and Eve they could eat the fruit of the trees of the garden; but of the tree which is in the midst of the garden, God said "Ye shall not eat of it, neither shall ye touch it, lest you die." This was the Gospel for Adam and Eve. Did this Gospel prove true? We know it did, because they both later died and death is still the result of sin !

We hear the same lie today that Satan told Eve and Adam, that we don't die, that our spirit lives and our eyes are opened, and we shall be as gods. After Eve ate and gave to Adam to eat which was forbidden, they became afraid and hid, and fear became part of mankind ! Satan preached the first sermon upon the immortality of the soul of man. We can hear this same sermon in many of the Churches today by Preachers who want to make people believe Satan's lie. Preachers preach this lie, that the spirit or soul returns to heaven to make people feel good, just as Satan wanted Eve to feel good ! We hear while some preacher's are having the funeral that the soul is already in heaven looking down on loved ones. Many people today believe this lie just as Eve believed Satan ! Many receive this lie as the Gospel, just as Eve did. Oh, if only Christians would read and search the Scriptures and know the Gospel of Truth for themselves and not depend on others for the Truth.

DOES THE GOSPEL INCLUDE GOD'S SABBATH DAY?

God has declared in His Word that the seventh day is a sign between Him and His chosen people—a sign of their loyalty. The seventh day is God's chosen day. He has not left this matter to be remodeled by priest or ruler. It is of too great importance to be left to human judgment. God saw that men would study their own convenience, and choose a day best suited to their own inclinations, a day bearing no divine authority; and He has stated plainly that the seventh day is the Sabbath of the Lord.

Men could not place themselves more decidedly in opposition to God's work and to His Law than by upholding a day that is without one evidence of sanctity, and professing to worship Him on that day. Those who have corrupted the Law by substituting a false sabbath for the holy Sabbath of God, and who compel the observance of this false sabbath, exalt themselves above God, and honor the spurious above the genuine.

Men have sought out many inventions. They have taken a common day, upon which God has placed no sanctity, and have clothed it with sacred prerogatives. They have declared it to be a holy day, but this does not give it a vestige of sanctity. They dishonor God by accepting human institutions and presenting to the world as the Christian Sabbath a day which has no "Thus saith the Lord" for its authority. Trust the Holy Scriptures, God's Word is eternal for all who are taken home to heaven will worship on God's Sabbath.

We hear and now urged to believe that the resurrection of

Christ from the Tomb and Cross on the first day of the week, made Sunday the Christian Sabbath. But Scripture evidence is lacking. The observance of Sunday as a Christian, had it's origin in that "mystery of lawlessness"—[2 Thess 2:7,RV.]. The only part of creation week that remains the same today, is the Sabbath that was blessed—the seventh-day and it will remain and be the same forever. How do we know? Isa 66:22-23—"For as the new heavens and the new earth, Which I will make shall remain before Me," says the Lord, "So shall your descendants and your name remain. And it shall come to pass That from one New Moon to another, and from one Sabbath to another, All flesh shall come to worship before Me." says the Lord.

We are not saved by works; for the Sabbath is not a work, it is a rest. It is denial for anyone to profess faith in God while ignoring or rejecting any Word of God. Man is to live by every Word that precedes out of the mouth of God.

God has compassion on the ignorant, and does not require that man should know a certain amount before they can be saved, but willful ignorance is a different thing. A person's ignorance may be the result of deliberately rejecting knowledge, and he that does that, rejects eternal life. For there is life in every Word of God. Every person will be brought to choose between the commandments of God and the commandments of men. All Christians will be divided into two great classes—those who keep the commandments of God and the faith of Jesus, and those who worship the beast and his image. From the first Sabbath in Eden to the present day, the knowledge of God's law has been preserved in the earth, and the Sabbath of the fourth commandment has been kept by people. Rev 14 in connection with the everlasting Gospel, will distinguish the Church of Christ at the time of His appearing. Rev 14:12—"Here is the patience of the saints; they are those who keep the commandments of God and the Faith of Jesus."

Many have reasoned that their family's have always kept Sunday, our fathers kept it, and many good people and pious men have died happy while keeping it. If they were right, so are we. They say that keeping the Sabbath would throw us out of harmony with the world, and we would have no influence over them. People think what can a little company keeping the seventh day hope to accomplish against all the world who are keeping Sunday? It was by similar arguments that the Jews endeavored to justify their rejection of Jesus Christ when He walked this earth. All the leaders of the people could not justify themselves or humble themselves to honor one, not like themselves. The same belief was held by the people before the flood that covered this earth ! Many today justify themselves as did the leaders of people when Christ walked this earth. Do people do this same thing today? It's hard for people to believe that so many people can be wrong about the day our Lord has asked us to honor and worship. The Sabbath commandment is the only commandment that God asked us to remember. God knew man would forget or worship on another day for a sabbath and wants us to know and remember the only part of Creation Week we have today !

The Sabbath brings hope and joy, in that it directs our mind to God, our Creator. Some may think, how can I make a living if I keep the Sabbath? The poor man may see in the Sabbath the solution of the problems of life. 1 Tim 4:8—"Godliness is profitable unto all things, having promise of the life now is, and that which is to come." There is a blessing when we honor God by resting the day He blessed and a different blessing of man's sabbath.

The Word of life that is proclaimed to us in the Gospel is that which was from the beginning. The Sabbath means triumphing in the works of God's hands, not in our hands. It means victory over sin and death, and everything connected with the curse of sin.

The Sabbath is a remnant of creation before the curse of sin came, and therefore those who keep it begins their eternal rest, for all who are saved will keep and honor God's Sabbath in heaven and the new earth. There is a Glorious Promise in Isa 58:13—14—"If thou turn away thy foot from the Sabbath, from doing thy own pleasure on My Holy Day; and call the Sabbath a delight, the Holy of the Lord, honorable; and shall honor Him, not doing thine own ways, nor finding thine own pleasure, nor speaking thine own words; then shalt thou delight thyself in the Lord; and I will cause thee to ride upon the high places of the earth, and feed thee with the heritage of Jacob thy father; for the mouth of the Lord hath spoken it." Eek 20:12 -"I gave them My Sabbaths to be a sign between Me and them, that they might know that I am the Lord that sanctify them." V-20—"And hollow My Sabbaths; and they will be a sign between Me and you, that you may know that I am the Lord your God."

God has given His Holy Law to the world as His measure of character. By this Law we may see and overcome every defect in our character and that we may have the Love of God in our lives that identifies us as His children and prepare us for the heavenly Kingdom with Jesus and all the heavenly angels.

The Sabbath is the seal of Creation, finished and perfect. the Sabbath reveals God as Creator and Sanctifier—Isa 20:12,20. The Gospel is about God, our Creator and what God wants His people to have and enjoy, but forever, eternity. "As the tree of knowledge was placed in the midst of the garden of Eden, so the Sabbath command is placed in the midst of the commandments." The tree of knowledge was the test of Adam's obedience, so the forth commandment is the test that God has given to prove the loyalty of all His people.

We know that the number seven is special to Christ and to the people who choose to accept the Gospel, which includes the

Law of God. Those who love the Law of the Lord will be taken to heaven when He comes. For a thousand years the saints will search the books to understand why some people chose not to accept the Gospel and are not in heaven. God is Love, and He will not force people against their will to accept His law of Love.

DOES THE GOSPEL INCLUDE
THE HISTORY OF THE WORLD?

The history of this world is found in God's Holy Bible. It is good for mankind to read and study the history of this earth. There has been only one kingdom of this world that was world wide. That Kingdom was the kingdom of Nebuchadnezzar's. There will never be another till Christ makes His Kingdom world wide. Jesus will be King, and His Kingdom will be ruled by "Love" for God and for one another. When will this take place? Scripture says—When all the professed church of Christ shall consent to be filled with God's Spirit. The whole world will soon hear the Gospel message in the fullness of its power, and the end will come for everyone, Some for eternal life and some for eternal death.

It is told that a non-Christian was boasting to a Christian, "We're going to destroy all the Christian churches and burn all your Bibles. We want leave you a thing to remind you of your God." The Christian said nothing. He only looked up toward the sky and smiled. The non believer was annoyed. Why are you smiling? "I'm just wondering" said the Christian, how you're going to get the star's down !

Thousands of years ago, the palmist wrote, "The heavens declare the glory of God, And the firmament shows His handiwork-Ps 19:1.

Job 26:7-14—Tells that God hangs the earth on nothing—bindeth up the waters in the thick clouds. Amos 4:13 —Tells Who formed the mountains, and creates the wind and reveals His thought to man, the One who makes the dawn out of darkness and strides on the heights of the earth. None other is there who can do as our God who formed mankind of the dust of the ground.

In sparing the life of Cain—Able's brother—the sons of Adam and Eve, God gave this world an example of what would be the results of permitting the sinner to live and continue a course of sin. Cain's descendants were led into sin, until the wickedness of man was so great, "Every imagination of the thought of his heart was only evil continually." "The earth also was corrupt before God, and the earth was filled with violence." Gen 6:11.

We read what this world and people will be like near the end, before Christ comes—2 Tim 3:1—5—"but know this, that in the last days perilous times will come; for men will be lovers of themselves, lovers of money, proud, blasphemers, disobedient to parents, unthankful, unholy, unloving, unforgiving, slanderers, without self-control, brutal, despisers of good, traitors, headstrong, haughty, lovers of pleasure rather than lovers of God, having a form of godliness but denying its power, and from such people turn away." V-7—"always learning and never able to come to the knowledge of the Truth."

Today is no different from the days Jesus walked this earth. Some people thought Jesus was confused. Others wrote Jesus off as an imposter, even a blasphemer—for Jesus did claim to be God. What do you and I think ? Our salvation depends on our choice.

THE GOSPEL SAYS A DAY IS COMING WHEN ALL WILL STAND BEFORE GOD

One day each person will say to God and all mankind, as all will stand before God,— "GUILTY or NOT GUILTY." The Law of heaven has been broken and the penalty of sin is death. No matter how much God loves us, He can't just say, "i forgive you" and except everyone into His Kingdom, because there would be so much confusion and people would not be happy. Heaven's perfect Law, the foundation of His universe, must be upheld. God can't downgrade His Law or disregard or change it or alter it or dispense with it—not even to save the life of His own Son !

So don't let anyone ever tell you that Jesus died on the cross, to do away with God's Law, "Ten Commandments" or were nailed to His cross. It is just the opposite. If the Law could have been changed or revised or over looked, then Jesus didn't need to have died, and Calvary was only a meaningless drama. Jesus died on the cross because there was no other way to save you and me—except to die in our place, because we have sinned and the wages of sin is eternal death. The one thing Christ has left to each person is the choice of obeying His Law of Love for Him and our fellow men and the choice of eternal life with Christ who came to this earth and suffered our punishment and death on the Cross. "The Gospel is about the Love of Jesus and what and why Jesus came to this earth and suffered and died in our place."

There is a story of a young woman who was given a ticket for speeding and brought before the Judge. The Judge read aloud the citation and said, "Guilty or not guilty to the young woman." She said Guilty. The Judge brought down his gavel and fined her one hundred dollars or ten days in jail. But he stood up, took off his robe. He walked around in front of the desk by the young woman, and paid her fine! This judge was her father. Why didn't the judge just say to his daughter, "You've broken the law, but I love you so much that I forgive you?" He couldn't do that and be a good Judge, a just Judge. He had to uphold the Law. But he could pay her fine himself. So it is with God. When heaven's law is broken, the penalty is death, not a hundred dollar fine. No matter how much God love's us, God can't say, "I forgive you, and let it go at that." Heaven's perfect law, the foundation of His universe, must be upheld. To do other wise would mean chaos. God couldn't downgrade His Law or disregard it or change it or overlook it—not even to save the life of His own Son.

So don't let anyone ever tell you that Jesus died on the cross to do away with the Law —God's Ten Commandments. It was just the opposite. If the Law could have been changed or overlooked, then Jesus didn't need to have died, and Calvary was only a meaningless drama. The wages of sin is death and all have sinned, but Jesus paid our debt, and for every person on earth. Each person that accepts what Jesus Christ has paid for with His life, will honor the Law of God.

Jesus died on the cross because there was no other way to save you and me. Jesus died in our place, for our sin that we have committed.

The Law of God, the sacrifice of Jesus on the cross for the sins of mankind is the "Gospel." What we do with this knowledge, will determine our life now and for eternity.

2 Thess 2:10—12 tells what those who choose not to obey the Gospel can look forward too.—"Those who perish because they did not receive the Love of the Truth, that they might be

saved. They will be condemned because they —had pleasure in unrighteousness." and for that reason God will send them strong delusion, that they should believe the lie, that they all may be condemned who did not believe the Truth, but believe and had pleasure in unrighteousness." The followers of Christ must tread the same path of humiliation, reproach, and suffering which their Master trod. The enmity that burst forth against the world's Redeemer will be manifested against all who should believe on His name.

A message was sent from heaven to the world in Noah's day, and their salvation depended upon the manner in which they treated this message. Because they rejected the warning, the Spirit of God was withdrawn from the sinful race, and they perished in the waters of the flood. In the time of Abraham, mercy ceased to plead with the guilty inhabitants of Sodom, and all but Lot with his wife and two daughters were consumed by the fire sent down from heaven. Coming to the last days, the same Infinite Power declares, concerning those who receive not the love of the Truth, that they might be saved; "For this cause God shall send them strong delusion, that they should believe a lie; that they all might be damned who believed not the Truth, but had pleasure in unrighteousness" 2 Thess 2:10-12. As people reject the teachings of the Gospel, God withdraws His Spirit and leaves them to the deceptions which they love. Christ still intercedes in man's behalf, and light will be given to those who seek it.

DOES THE GOSPEL
REVEAL SIN?

The predicament of mankind is that we are caught in the ropes of sin in this world. We can't get away from sin, it is every where we go and every where we look. But, yes we do have something that can set us free. it is the "Gospel" the Word of the living God, which is sharper than any two—edged sword—Heb 4:12. God's Book—Holy Bible—is powerful, full of promises for you and me. These promises can be claimed by faith, these promises are the Gospel of God.

What if God wasn't the same all the time for this world / Heb 13:8—"Jesus Christ the same yesterday, today, and forever." We can depend on God, who gave us physical laws that govern our universe and allow us to live safely but also spiritual laws that give us life in Him—"eternal life". For those who have accepted the salvation offered by our Savior, it isn't so important when our earthly life may come to a close. Eternal life lies ahead. Life forever with Jesus and our loved ones where life will never end.

The first step in coming to Christ is to acknowledge sin in our life. What is sin? 1 John 3:4—"Whosoever commits sin, also commits lawlessness, and sin is Lawlessness." Gods law is a mirror which shows the perfection of a righteous character and enables us to discern the defects in our life. Gods Law reveals to man his sins, but provides no remedy. The Gospel of Christ alone can free one from the condemnation of sin. We must exercise repentance toward God and have faith in Christ, His atoning sacrifice for our sins. We may conceal our sins from the eyes of men, but we can hide nothing from our Creator God. The will of God is expressed in the precepts of His Holy Law. The Law of God is not rendered in the spirit of legality, only "Love".

Paul asks in Rom 3:31—"Do we then make void the Law through faith? God forbids, yea, we establish the Law." God's Law reveals to man his sins, but it provides no remedy. the Gospel of Christ alone can free people from the condemnation or the defilement of sin. Ps 19:7—"The Law of the Lord is perfect, converting the soul." without the Law, man has no conception of the purity and Holiness of God or of their own guilt, we have no true conviction of sin and feel no need of repentance.

Christ prayed for His disciples—John 17:17—"Sanctify them through Thy Truth; the Word of Truth." What is Truth? Ps 119:142—"Thy Law is the Truth." V-151—"All Thy commandments are Truth." V-160—"Thy Word is true from the beginning—and endures forever."

Many today profess to accept Jesus the Son of God and to believe in His death and resurrection, but they have no conviction of sin and feel no need of repentance or of a change of heart. It is only because of the spirit of compromise with sin, that the great truths of the word of God are so differently regarded. Why? Because there is so little vital godliness in the churches, because Christianity is apparently so popular with the world. In place of the requirements of God, the church has substituted human theories and traditions.

THE POWER OF THE GOSPEL OF GOD

The Gospel is power from God. There is this story of a forest fire that swept through and destroyed property and a little home at the edge of the woods. When the owner returned from work, he met this horrible sight. He went out to where the chicken coop had been. It, too was a mass of ashes. At his feet lay a mound of charred feathers. He kicked it over, what do you suppose happened? Four little fussy babies scrambled out. Four little baby chicks survived by their mother's love. Every thing our God created has love in it. Why did this mother Hen protect her babies, we find the answer in God's word, 1 John 4:8—"He who does not love does not know God, for God is Love." Everything God has created has love in them, but He does not force love because then it would not be 'love'. Friend, do you want to be covered when fire sweeps this earth? You can be ! You can be sheltered by your Creator Savior ! Trust the gospel of God and His Love. It's amazing that the world today can't accept the Truth of the Gospel. In 1968, Astronauts Frank Borman, James Lovell, and William Anders read to the world from outer space, orbiting the moon in "Apollo 8", the first chapter of the Old Testament "Bible", somehow familiar and yet nearly forgotten: "IN THE BEGINNING GOD CREATED THE HEAVENS AND THE EARTH>" Do you believe that our Creator God would create this world and not have a Law for the well being of His creation ? God has given people today directions and laws for the well being of His Creation. These directions are found in His Book, written by people inspired by God. This Book is His Holy Bible.

Life on this earth is short compared to what our Creator God has offered every person He has created. A story of a father and his son illustrates mankind today. This son of a farmer was well educated, went to college and studied agriculture and came home to help his father with the farm. His father said, Son, I'm getting old, I'm ready to retire and there is one stipulation I want you to run the farm strictly according to my directions for the first year. After that the farm will be yours.

The Son said that's fair enough. The two men spent the next few days going from field to field as what was to be planted in each field. The son, Bill wrote in his notebook what his dad wanted planted in each field. Bill the son used his soil testing kit on each field on the farm. Bill was impressed with his father's wisdom. Every time his father had chosen the very crop, according to what Bill had learned in college to plant in each field.

Overtime—until the last field, his father had said to plant corn, but he must have made a mistake the son thought. Bill thought the field would be perfect for peanuts. Bill knew his dad would be pleased to see that all the money spent on education had paid off. Bill planted peanuts.

Dad came back at harvest time, and said the farm had never looked so good. Bill took his Dad around and showed him the wheat and potatoes and alfalfa. "But where is the corn, Dad wanted to know.? I thought I told you to plant corn. Bill said, "Well, yes Dad, that was in the field over there. I went back and tested the soil in all the fields. You were exactly right in all the fields except this one, so I thought you must have made a mistake. I was sure you would rather see a good crop of peanuts than a sickly crop of corn. Do people do the same today? Do what they think rather than what we have been asked by our Heavenly Father?

Dad shook his head sadly, "Bill, he said, you haven't followed my directions in any of these fields. You've followed your 'own' judgment in every case." It just happened that you agreed with me in all points except one. But as soon as there was any question, you did what "you" thought was best in spite of what I had directed you to do. I'm sorry, Son, but you'll have to look else where for a farm of your own. Do people do the same today?

What do you think? Was the father to harsh? Or, was he absolutely right? Does it mean anything at all to follow directions—especially when they are from God's Book "Bible" or only when we agree with His Gospel? Our Father has given us directions in His Holy Bible, specific directions, He wrote them on stone, that we follow them, and not try to change them. God promises not a farm but a future beyond our dreams, and a never ending life.

But if we agree only when we agree with what God has written, have we obeyed at all ? Matt 7:21—"Not everyone who says to Me, Lord, Lord, shall enter the kingdom of heaven, but he who does the will of My Father in heaven." What part of the Gospel do you and I choose, the part that we like or all parts ?

CAN THE GOSPEL
CHANGE A PERSON?

Things change in the world today. Flowers fade and die and are replaced with weeds. Wells go dry, Worship, once sincere and fresh, become's only a hollow form. Today, people are aligning themselves, either following the Gospel of our Creator or going their own way which leads to eternal death. Proverbs 16:28—"There is a way that seems right to a man. But its end is the way of death." While we cannot depend on anyone on this earth for survival, we can depend on the One who created our world and everything good in it. God has said, "I will be with you, I will not leave you or forsake you. Don't be afraid."—Deuteronomy 31:8. Ps 89:34—"I will not violate My covenant or change what My lips have said." Isa 31:2—"God does not go back on what He says." Mal 3:6—"I have not changed." Why do we hear today about the Sabbath that God created the week of creation is now the first day of the week ? Do we believe what God has said in His Holy Bible or do we believe what Satan has inspired mankind to proclaim? Deuteronomy 11:27—"There will be a blessing if you obey the commands of our Lord." Deut 12:32—"Do what I command you, don't add nor take away anything." Prov 19:16—"The one who keeps My commandments preserves himself."

If you have never accepted Christ's offer of forgiveness and eternal life, perhaps He is asking you to make that decision right now. There will never be a better time. Only as we realize who it was that died for our sins—it is only then we begin to realize what our forgiveness cost, the value of the salvation made possible on the cross, the gift that is now ours for asking !

How much of God's Gospel do we need in our life? Can I have just a little religion in me? Selfishness must be overcome, and God will work for you and in you. Some want God to be their copilot, but don't give God permission to direct their life. Nothing is so fulfilling in your life than to surrendering your life to God. In 'Truth', God brings excitement, vision, and fulfillment. What can the Gospel do for you?

1. —A Thief—to a giving person in need.
2. —A unforgiving person—peace and forgiveness.
3. —A Confused person—now with a purpose in life.
4. —A Critical person—understanding person
5. —A Arrogant person—to a humble person.
6. —Afraid person—Bold
7. —A person afraid to witness—to a bold person.
8. —A lonely person—to a person loved by the King of the Universe.
9. —A worried person—to trusting in our Creator God.
10. — A fearful person —to a peaceful calm person.
11. —A Broken and depressed person—to a person of joy for what God has in store for those who Love and obey Him.
12. —A shameful person—to a proud child of God.
13. —A person deceived into sin—to a forgiven and free person.

Does any of these describe your life? Accept the Lord's Gospel and be free !

"The work of righteousness shall be peace and the effect will be, Quietness and assurance forever"r—Isa 32:17. He who obeys the divine Law will most truly respect and obey the laws of his country. He who fears God will honor the King in the exercise of all just and legitimate authority.

True freedom lies within the proscriptions of the Law of God. Isa 48:18—"Oh, that you had heeded My commandments! Then your peace would have been like a river, and your righteousness as the waves of the sea." Prov 1:33—"But whoever listens to Me will dwell safely, and will be secure without fear of evil."

LOVE IS THE HEART OF THE GOSPEL

Biblical Love is a matter of choice. Love is more than just something we say. Love is something we do ! Love is living the Gospel of Christ, which is love for our Creator God and for our fellow man. People today are no different from Israel of old. The people of Israel mocked the messenger of God, and despised God's Words, and misused His prophets, until the wrath of the Lord arose against these people—. 2 Chron 36:15-16. The same spirit that actuated the Jewish people 'Israel' to want to be like the heathen people around them, and reject God, was because they thought they could manage things better themselves. This same spirit has come upon the world today. We need to look no father than the representatives of the people in our nation. Many deny there is a Creator God ! Jeremiah 2:19—"Know therefore and see that it is an evil and bitter thing to forsake the Lord your God." This is the same policy which has been pursued in all ages. Elijah was declared to be a troubler in Israel, Jeremiah a traitor, Paul a polluter of the temple. From that day to this, those who would be loyal to truth have been denounced as seditious, heretical, or schismatic. This spirit will increase as the close of time comes upon this world. The great obstacle both to the acceptance and to the promulgation of truth is the fact that it involves inconvenience and reproach. This is the only argument against the truth which its advocates have never been able to refute, Those who do not wait for Truth to become popular are the true followers of the Gospel. We should choose Truth because it is Truth and leave the consequences with God. Isa 51:7-8—"hearken unto Me, ye that know righteousness, the people in whose heart is My Law; fear ye not the reproach of men, neither be ye afraid of their reviling. For the moth shall eat them up like a garment, and the worm shall eat them like wool; but My righteousness shale be forever, My salvation from generation to generation."

Believing God's Word "Gospel" we come from bondage of pride and self-confidence, to the freedom of God's gentleness. Who will heed God's call, and exchange the bondage of sin, human traditions and speculations for the freedom which God's eternal Word of Truth gives? Acts 10:34-35—"God is no respecter of persons, but in every nation he that fears Him and works righteousness, is accepted with Him." We do not earn salvation by our obedience, for salvation is the free gift of God, to be received by faith. If we abide in Christ, if the love of God dwells in us, our feelings, our thoughts, our purposes, our actions, will be in harmony with the will of God as expressed in the precepts of Gods Holy Law.

1 John 4:8—"He who does not love does not know God, for God is Love." 1 John 5:17—"all unrighteousness is sin, and there is sin not leading to death." We ask how can this be ? Christ will forgive sin when we ask forgiveness and turn away from sin. God is faithful and just to forgive us when we ask and turn away from our sin !

Opportunities extend to everyone who has received the light of Truth to warn other's what is to come upon this world. The great obstacle is the fact that it involves inconvenience and reproach. But this does not deter the true followers of Christ. True followers do not wait for truth to become popular. We should choose the truth because it is right, and leave the consequences with God.

The person who does not love the Law of God does not love the gospel, for the law, as well as the gospel is a mirror reflecting the true character of God. Thus the Gospel loses its value and importance in the mind of people, soon as they cast away the Law of God. The Law of God is the foundation of the government of God. Love to God and love to our neighbor constitute the whole duty of man. Love to God and love to man will give the clear title to heaven. What evidence have we that we have the pure love, without alloy? God has erected a standard that we may know, His commandments. John 14:21—"He that hath My commandments, and keeps them, he it is that loveth Me."

Many religious teachers and preachers say that Christ by His death abolished His Law, and men are henceforth free from its requirements. This claim that Christ by His death abolished His Father's Law is without foundation. Had it been possible for the Law to have been changed or set aside, then Christ need not have died to save man from the penalty of sin. Jesus Christ came and died for the sins of every person that has sinned, that the Law may be fulfilled, for every person has sinned that has ever lived from creation. Jesus said in Matt 5: 17-18 —"Do not think that I came to destroy the Law or the prophets: I did not come to destroy but to fulfill. for assuredly, I say unto you, "till heaven and earth pass away, one jot or one tittle will by no means pass from the Law till all be fulfilled." V-19—"Whoever therefore breaks one of the least of these commandments and teaches men so, shall be called least in the kingdom of heaven, but he that does them and teaches them, he shall be called great in the kingdom of heaven." God's Law is a law of Love, revealing that love is the fulfilling of God's Law. Ps 119:142, 172—"Thy law is the truth"—all Thy commandments are righteousness." God's Law reveals our sins, but it does not provide a remedy. How do we show our love to God ? 1John 5:3—"This is the love of God, that we keep His commandments, and His commandments are not grievous." Psalms 19:7—"The Law of the Lord is perfect, converting the soul." Let none deceive themselves with the belief that they can become Holy while willfully violating one of God's requirements. ! John 2:4—"He that saith, I know Him, and does not keep His commandments is a liar, and the truth is not in him." Scripture reveals the claims are without foundation if we don't honor and keep the Law of God.

The same spirit that prompted rebellion in heaven still inspires rebellion on earth today. Reproof of sin still arouses the spirit of hatred and resistance. From the days of righteous Able to our own time, such is the spirit which has been displayed toward those who dare to condemn sin. God gave us evidence of His Love by yielding up His only-begotten Son to die for the fallen race.

How long would a marriage last if one of the two were to keep seeing others that are popular among society? When we vow to honor our marriage vow, we should keep that promise. Does God require less ? When we vow to honor our Creator, we have a certificate in Scripture that we vow to honor. This certificate is the only thing that helps us to be faithful to our vow. There is only ten ways to honor our vow, and it's found in the Word of God—called "God's Ten Commandments"—Exodus 20:1—17. What evidence have we that we have pure Love, without alloy ? John 14:21—"He that hath My commandments, and keepeth them, he it is that loveth Me."

DOES THE GOSPEL REQUIRE NATIONAL RELIGION AND ONE CHURCH?

The idea of a national Church and national Religion is wonderful, fascinating, because it is so much more pleasant for people to suppose that they are to be saved in bulk, regardless character, instead of through faith and righteousness. 1 Samuel 16:7—"Man looks on the outward appearance, but the Lord looks at the heart."

Babylon is said to be the mother of harlots. By this we know her daughters must be symbolized churches that cling to her doctrines and traditions, and follow her example of sacrificing the Truth of the Gospel, in order to form an unlawful alliance with the world.

Many of the Protestant Churches are following Babylon's example of iniquitous connection, by seeking the favor of the world. The term 'Babylon' which means "confusion" may be appropriately applied to these churches, for all profess to derive their doctrines from the Holy Bible, yet divided into almost 'innumerable sects',with widely conflicting creeds and theories. Some claim their church is from the root of Christendom with equal right, to be the original. others say we should find the name of the true church in the Bible. Now many names are given to the Christians in the New Testament; the Church of God; The Church of Christ; Followers of the Way; and others. God identified His true people by their faith and doctrines; Those who "keep the commandments of God and have the Spirit of Prophecy." God tells us how we might know whether they are true followers of Christ. Isaiah 8:20—"To the Law and to the testimony, if they speak not according to this Word, it is because there is no light in them." Try them. If they teach according to the Bible, believe them. If they don't speak according to the Law and according to the Bible, there is no light in them.

At the turn of the 19th century all churches came to believe in the second coming of Christ. This wasn't some branch off some other church. It was a spontaneous revival and reformation of the faith once delivered to the saints. People from all churches—Baptists, Methodists, Christians, Congregationalists, Catholics and all kinds of people came together at once and became known as Adventists because they believed in the Second coming of Jesus Christ. Webster's defines Adventists as those looking for the coming of the Lord to earth which included people of all the different churches in the year 1844. They studied their Bibles to be sure they hadn't left out truth. Together they began to preach this message and in just over one short hundred years this message has gone to almost every country in the world.

The great sin charged against Babylon is she made all the nations drink of the wine—"Teachings"— of the wrath of her fornication. Babylon exerts a corrupting influence upon the world by teaching doctrines which are opposed to the plainest statements of Holy Writ, "Gospel". Religious faith appears so confused and discord of what is taught as the Gospel in the different churches, people know not what to believe as Truth ! The sin of the world's impenitence lies at the door of the churches ! The Gospel is simple enough for every person on earth to understand, the Gospel of God is Love for Christ and our fellow man.

In the first centuries the true Sabbath had been kept by all Christians. They were jealous for the honor of God, and believing that His Law is immutable, they zealously guarded the sacredness of its precepts. Satan worked through his agents to bring about his object. Satan's object was to destroy God's Sabbath. Sunday's made a festival day in honor of the resurrection of Christ. Religious services were held upon it; yet it was regarded as a day of recreation, the Sabbath being still sacredly observed. Satan then cast contempt upon the Sabbath of creation as a Jewish institution. The day of the sun was reverenced by Satan's pagan subjects and was honored by Christians. The emperor's policy thinking to unite the conflicting interests of heathenism and Christianity, he would promote the heathen to unite with Christians and advance the power and glory of the church. Many God-fearing Christians were gradually led to regard Sunday as possessing a degree of sacredness, but they still honored the true Sabbath as the Holy of the Lord and observed it in obedience to the forth commandment of God. Thus the pagan festival came finally to be honored as a divine institution, while the Bible Sabbath was pronounced a relic of Judaism, and its observers were declared to be accursed.

The only one of the commandments God says to remember is the forth commandment and the world has forgotten this commandment more than any of the Ten ! Why? This commandment reveals the Creator of the heavens and the earth. This commandment was designed to keep the living God ever before the minds of men as the source of being and the object of reverence and worship. This commandment points to God as Creator of heaven and earth.

In Some churches —'Pastors now' urge that the resurrection of Christ on Sunday made it the Christian Sabbath. But Scripture evidence is lacking. The Gospel Truth on God's Sabbath was lost sight of, but the forms of religion were multiplied, and the people are burdened with rigorous exactions today.

The words of Christ to His disciples are applicable to His followers to the close of time, till Christ comes. We see today, the result of the church's departing from the Gospel of Truth, and ally themselves more closely with the world, that many are departing and connecting with those who are lover's of pleasure more than lovers of God. Scripture tells of these today—2 Tim 3:5—"Having a form of godliness, but denying the power there of; from such turn away."

Religion has become the sport of infidels and skeptics, because many who bear it's name are ignorant of its principles. The power of Godliness has well-nigh departed from many of our churches. Picnics, church theatricals, church fairs, fine homes, personal display, having banished thought's of God. Things of eternal interest receive hardly a passing notice. We hear from many religious teachers that Christ at His death abolished His Law, and men henceforth are free from its requirements. In contrast to the bondage of the law, they present the 'liberty' to be enjoyed under the Gospel. The death of Christ, so far from abolishing the Law, proves that it is immutable. Isa 42:21—"The Lord is well pleased for His righteousness sake; He will magnify the Law, and make it honorable." While on earth Christ said, Matt 5:17—"Think not that I come to destroy the Law, or the prophets; I am not come to destroy, but to fulfill." What does fulfill mean? Webster's dictionary explains this as —"to carry out—to do something required—obey." Did Jesus Christ obey the Law while on earth? Why does mankind think to change part of the Law of God, or is it Satan who wants to annul The Law of God and the Gospel ? Every commandment in the Law of God express's how to Love God and our fellow man. Rom 13:10—"Love is the fulfilling of the Law." Ps 119:142—"Thy Law is the Truth." V-172—"for all Thy commandments are righteousness."

As time gets closer to the end of this world, sin will be more manifest and our churches will try to appeal to the civil powers to unite all churches. As the movement for Sunday worship enforcement becomes more bold and decided, the law will be invoked against commandment keepers. But the steadfast answer of the true Christians will be, "Show us from the Word of God our error." The same plea was made by Martin Luther to the authorities under similar circumstances. Those that will take their stand before the courts, and before the thousands of people will be heard by many for the first time, the Gospel Truth in God's Word who otherwise would know nothing of these truths. Many people have never heard about the Gospel of God's Sabbath and laws for people to live by. No person can serve God without enlisting against themselves the opposition of the hosts of evil.

The Gospel of Truth will be carried not so much by argument as by the deep conviction of the Spirit of God. Truth is more precious than all besides. Many who have combined their efforts against the Truth, will take their stand upon the Lord's side when they hear the Gospel Truth for the first time. There is no better time to surrender your life to God than today.

THE GOSPEL OF WHOM
WE WORSHIP

Many people who want to come to Christ and worship as asked in Scripture, do not know what the Lord desires of us. We can find the answer in Rev 14:7—"Fear God, and give glory to Him and worship Him the Creator of the heavens and the earth." How do we do this today? We are told in Ecclesiastes 12:13—"Fear God, and keep His commandments, for this is the whole duty of man." 1 John 5:3—"for this is the Love of God, that we keep His commandments; and His commandments are not grievous." Proverbs 28:9—"One who turns away his ear from hearing the Law, even his prayers shall be abomination." 1John 2:4—'He that saith, I know Him, and does not keep His commandments, is a liar, and the Truth is not in him."

There are but two religions in the world. One class of religions are those which men have invented, in all of which man saves himself by ceremonies and good works; the other is that one religion which is revealed in the Bible, which teaches people to look for salvation solely from the free Grace of God. The Bible is the only infallible authority in religion. Only by the Bible can people arrive at the 'truth and Gospel'.

The Rabbis warned the people while Jesus was on earth against receiving the new doctrines taught by Jesus, for His theories and practices were contrary to the teachings of the fathers. People gave credence to what the priest and Pharisees taught, rather than to understand the Word of God for themselves. People honored the priest and the rulers instead of honoring God, and rejected the truth so that they might keep their own traditions. Do people do the same today? It is hard to break away from traditions we have followed in our lives for generations. But we all are looking for a better life to come with Jesus.

Think about who has promised a better life to those who Love their Creator God. He was driven from Bethlehem by a jealous King, rejected by His own people of the church He grew up in - Nazareth. He was condemned to death without a cause at Jerusalem. He, who healed the sick, restored sight to the blind, hearing to the deaf, and speech to the dumb, who fed the hungry, comforted the sorrowful, was driven from the people He labored to save. He walked upon heaving billows, and by a word silenced the angry roaring water, cast out devils, who broke the slumbers of the dead, and held thousands entranced by His words of wisdom, but was not able to reach the hearts of those who were blinded by prejudice and hatred, and who stubbornly rejected the "Truth". the choice is still to be made by each person today. Only the choice made from 'Love' is of value.

The duty to worship God is based upon the fact that God is our Creator and that to Him all other beings owe their existence. We can read that God created mankind in Gen 1:26— and we were created in God's image and likeness. V-27—"God created both male and female. God created all that was made in six days and, it was very good-V-31.

All that was created was done in six days by God and God ended His work and on the seventh day He rested from all His work. Gen 2:3—"Then God blessed the seventh day and sanctified it." God wants mankind to know the truth about His creation and how and why He created a Seventh-day just to rest and worship Him. The keeping of the Sabbath is a sign of loyalty to the only true God and Creator.

In the last book of Scripture Rev 14:7—"Fear God, and give

glory to Him—worship Him that made heaven, and earth, and sea, and the fountains of water." The keeping of the Sabbath is our sign of loyalty to the only true God.

The Declaration of Independence set forth a great truth that "all men are created equal." Freedom of religious faith was also granted, every person being permitted to worship God according to the dictates of his conscience. The day will come when a false church will try to force people to worship on a false sabbath. The false church will have a form of godliness, but denying the power there of—2 Tim 3:1-5.

The worshipers of God will be especially distinguished by their regard for the forth commandment, since this is the sign of God's creative power. The false worshipers will be distinguished by their efforts to tear down our Creator's memorial of His creation. Man has tried, with arrogant claims to compel the observance of the first day of the week—Sunday"—as the Lord's day. But the Bible points to the seventh day, and not to the first day, as the Lord's day. Isa 58:13—calls the Sabbath —"My Holy Day." Some have claimed that Christ changed the Sabbath but is disproved by His own words in Matt 5:17—"think not that I am come to destroy the Law, or the prophets; I am not come to destroy, but to fulfill." V-18—"Till heaven and earth pass, one jot or one tittle shall in no wise pass from the Law, till all be fulfilled."

Christians of the past generations observed Sunday supposing that in so doing they were keeping the Sabbath; and there are still true Christian's in every Church, including the Roman Catholic communion, who honestly believe that Sunday is the Sabbath of divine appointment. God accepts their sincerity of purpose and their integrity before Him. But when Sunday observance shall be enforced by Law, and the world shall be enlightened concerning the obligation of the true Sabbath, then who ever shall transgress the command of God, will thereby honor popery above God. It is not until this issue, is thus plainly set before the people, and they are brought to choose between the commandments of God or the commandments of men, that those who continue in transgression will have made their choice to whom they will obey. Those who understanding the claims of the forth commandment, and choose to observe the false instead of the true Sabbath are thereby paying homage to that power by which alone it is commanded. All Christians will be divided into two classes, those who keep the commandments of God, and those who worship and honor Satan.

From the days when God proclaimed His Law, to the assembled multitude at Sinai, the knowledge of God's Law has been preserved in the earth, and the Sabbath has been kept.

Rev 14 tells about the company of people that will make up those whom God will redeem from the earth. V-14—"Here is the patience of the saints; here are they that keep the commandments of God, and the faith of Jesus." The ever lasting Gospel will distinguish the church of Christ at the time of Christ appearing.

Many people today urge that Sunday keeping has been an established doctrine and a widespread custom of the church for many centuries. It is shown that the Sabbath and it's observance are more ancient and widespread, even as old as the world itself, and bearing the sanction both of angels and God. The Sabbath was ordained by no human authority and rest upon no human traditions; it was established by the Ancient of Days and commanded by His eternal Word. This part of the Gospel will stand the test of time for eternity !

Scripture tells that —Isa 4:1—"Seven women wanting to be called by the Lord's name, but do as they please." Do we see this today? Women in scripture are the symbol of churches who follow Christ or should !

All will by our own choice decide their destiny. Christians that love Jesus better than the world will love to speak of Jesus, their best Friend. Consider that the pleasures of this earth will have an end, and that which we sow, we must also reap. We may conceal our sins from the eyes of men, but we can hide nothing from our Creator. The work of preparation for heaven is an individual work. We are not saved in groups, or having our names on the Church membership list.

All who have truly repented of sin, and by faith claimed he blood of Jesus Christ as their atoning sacrifice, have pardon entered against their names in the books of heaven. Their sins will be blotted out. Isa 43:25.

THE GOSPEL OF THE
NEW COVENANT

Our Lord has promised to make a new covenant with His people—Isa 31:33—"I will put My Law in their inward parts, and write it in their heart, and I will be their God, and they shall be My people, and they shall teach no more every man his neighbor, and every man his brother, saying know the Lord; for they shall all know Me, from the least of them unto the greatest of them; saith the Lord; for I will forgive their iniquity, and I will remember their sin no more."

When God came to Mt Sinai, the Mountain shook when Good spoke. When God makes the new covenant with those whom God saves, the whole earth will shake. The Lord Himself will descend from heaven with a shout, with the voice of the Archangel, and with the trump of God—Ps 50:3. ! These 4:16— "the dead in Christ shall rise first." Matt 16:27—"The Lord will reward every person according to their work." Matt 25:31—"The Lord shall come in His glory." Rev 50:3—"The Lord will not be silent."

The first dominion of God will be restored. Let no one think to excuse himself from keeping the commandments of God, by saying that he is under the new covenant. Whoever rejoices in the promises of the new covenant, the blessings of which the Holy Spirit even now makes real, must remember that it is the virtue of the new covenant that the Law of God is put into our hearts. The old covenant brought no one to the obedience of the Law, but the new covenant makes it universal, so that the earth shall be full of the knowledge of the Lord, as the waters cover the sea.

Thanks be unto God for His unspeakable gift ! Isa 40:8—"The grass withers, the flower fades; but the Word of our God shall stand forever." Isa 66:22—"For as the new heavens and the new earth, which I will make, shall remain before Me, saith the Lord, so shall your seed and your name remain."

Read the promises of God in Rev 21—"How God will bring the tabernacle of God from heaven to be with men, and dwell with them—and God Himself shall be with them, and be their God." "There shall be neither death, neither sorrow, nor crying—nor pain; for the former things are passed away," V-4. "Blessed are they that do His commandments, that they may have right to the tree of life, and may enter in through the gates into the city" Rev 22:14. Friend, all the Gospel of God is in His "Ten Commandments" showing us how we are to honor our Creator and how to love our fellow man as ourselves. The Gospel is not for a few chosen people, but for every person on earth.

There will be people saved who never heard the Gospel. God has revealed to them that there is a Creator God of mankind. Man did not come from a big bang and develop through millions of years as some may believe. How do we know that there will be people saved that did not know about the gospel? Because these people knew in their heart that righteousness and evil does exist in this world. Zechariah 13:6—"And one will say to Him. 'What are these wounds between your arms? Then He will answer, 'Those with which I was wounded in the house of My friends." We know that Rehab the harlot knew in her heart that there is a God who provides for those who love and obey Him. Rehab is of the family that the decedents of Mary, the mother of Jesus was born. Jesus has a family and wants to be reunited with His family and all those that Love Him and honor the Law that all heaven live's by. When we hear a message presented to God's people, we should not rise up in opposition to it, we should go to our Bible, comparing it with the Law and testimony's, and if it bares not the Bible test, it is not true—Isa 8:20; —Galatians 3:24.

THE GOSPEL OF THE COMING CRISIS

The Spirit of God is withdrawing from this earth, and calamity follows calamity by sea and by land. There are earthquakes, fires, floods, murder's of every grade. Rapidly people are placing themselves under the banner they have chosen. i appeal to all members of all churches not to disregard the fulfilling of the signs of our times, which say so plainly that we are near the end of this world.

From the beginning of the great controversy in heaven, it has been Satan's purpose to overthrow the Law of God. After Satan was cast out of heaven, he has continued the same warfare upon earth. Whether this be accomplished by casting aside the Law altogether, or by rejecting one of its precepts, the result is the same. James 2:10—"Who ever shall keep the whole law, and yet offend in one point, he is guilty of all." Satan has so perverted the doctrines of the Bible, errors have thus become incorporated into the faith of millions who profess to believe the Gospel. Christians have accepted tradition and fables as the Gospel. Whenever the Law of God is rejected, sin ceases to appear sinful or the Gospel desirable. Those who teach Christians to regard lightly the commandments of God sow disobedience to reap disobedience.

The doctrine that men are released from obedience to God's commandments has weakened man's moral obligation to one another and to God. To destroy faith in the Bible serves Satan's purpose as well as to destroy the Bible itself. Satan works harder through the Church to further his delusions for Christians. Satan's doctrine that he has brought into the Christian world, that eternal torment has led many to disbelieve the Bible. Satan uses popular preachers and teachers to declare that the law of God is no longer binding or required to be a disciple of Christ.

The gospel of Satan is, that the Law of God is no longer part of the Gospel, Satan has weakened the force of moral obligation and opened the floodgates of iniquity upon the world. This fast spreading corruption is largely attributable to forsaking the Law of God, the desecration of the Christian Sabbath." and the enforcement of Sunday, and those who refuse to unite with the new sabbath are denounced as the enemies of reform.

The line of distinction between professed Christians and the ungodly is now hardly distinguishable. Church members love what the world loves and are ready to join with them in body to strengthen their cause.

Satan will bring trouble upon people and lead men to believe that it is God who is afficting them. The Scripture records how Satan afflicted Job, how quickly Satan destroyed flocks, herds, servants, houses, and children. One trouble succeeded another as in a moment. God shielded Job's life and God can shield you !

Today we see where Satan brings disease and disaster on cities, accidents and calamities by sea and by land and in the air. We see tornadoes and terrific hailstorms, floods, cyclones, fires, tidal waves and earthquakes in every place on earth. We are told in 2 Tim 3:12—"All that live Godly in Christ Jesus shall suffer persecution." The hope Christians have is beyond all these things coming on the earth. "Jesus is coming soon !

The day is coming that as Ahab in Scripture told Elijah he was the one who was to blame for all the trouble in Israel. The world will again blame those who honor the Law of God, to be the cause of the world's trouble. The world will follow the same policy of deception as did the angels in heaven did when Satan revolted and claimed that there was no need for God's Law. Do we hear the same today? We are to guard against dishonoring God and His Law, by professing to be His people, and then going directly contrary to God's Law.

God never forces the will or the conscience, but Satan's constant resort to gain control of those he cannot seduce, is compulsion by cruelty. Though fear or force Satan endeavors to rule our conscience. To accomplish this, Satan works through both religious and secular authorities, moving them to the enforcement of human laws in defiance of the Law of God.

The exercise of force is contrary to the principles of God's government. God desires only service of Love; and love cannot be commanded; it cannot be won by force or authority. Only by love is love awakened. To know God is to Love Him and our fellow man.

Satan will use Ministers to deny the obligation of the divine law and encourage people to yield obedience to the civil authorities as ordained of God. As the Protestant churches reject the clear, Scripture Gospel in defense of God's Law, they will long to silence those whose faith cannot be overthrown by the Bible. We see today how Political corruption is destroying love of justice and regard for the Gospel of Truth in America. The Gospel in Scripture is a safeguard against the influence of the false teachers. None but those who have fortified their minds with the Truth of the Bible will stand through the last great conflict.

Satan is constantly endeavoring to attract attention to man in the place of God. He leads people to look to bishops, to Pastors, to professors of theology, as their guides, instead of searching the Scriptures to learn their duty for themselves. The Holy Scriptures is full of warnings against false teachers. There are today millions who profess religion who can give no answer or reason for the points of their faith than that they were so instructed by their religious teachers. People pass by the teachings of Jesus and place confidence in the words of their ministers, but are ministers infallible ? God has given us His Word that we may become acquainted with His teachings and know for ourselves what God requires of us. We have the Bible so acceptable to every person today and yet so neglected by those who pretend to be followers of truth of what the Bible teaches. Every person has the opportunity to have a Bible and know for themselves the Gospel of Truth. Oh, that Christians would take time to study what God has given us in His Word !

it was not the scholarly theologians who had an understanding of this Truth, and engaged in its proclamation of the coming of Christ to earth to die for the sins of the world. The leaders then were so absorbed in their ambitious for place and power among men, they lost sight of the divine honors of proclaiming the coming of Christ, the King of heaven. God committed the Gospel to the Jewish leaders; but they were without excuse, they did not know and declare to the people that the Messiah's coming was at hand. Their ignorance was the result of sinful neglect.

The greatest event in the world's history, was the coming of the Son of God to accomplish the redemption of mankind. And no doors were open to receive Him. Had the leaders of the church been faithful to they're calling, all the people should have known and watching and waiting, that they might be among the first to welcome the world's Redeemer. Angels were appointed to carry the glad tidings to those who were prepared to receive the message and who would joyfully make it known to the world. There were also in the land of the heathen, those that looked for the Son of God; they were wise men, rich and noble, the philosophers of the East. As it is unto them that looked for Christ the first time. It is unto them that are looking for Christ to come the second time that He will appear without sin unto salvation—Heb 9:28. Like the tidings of our Savior's birth, the message of the second advent was not committed to the religious leaders of the people. They had failed to preserve their connection with God, and had refused light from heaven; therefor they were not of the number described by the apostle Paul; "But ye, brethren, are not in darkness, that the day should overtake you as a thief. Ye are all the children of the light, and the children of the day; we are not of the night, nor of darkness."—1Thess 5:4-5.

It's not enough to have good intentions, it is not enough to do what a person thinks is right or what the ministers tell what he thinks is right. Your soul's salvation is at stake and we need to search the Scriptures ourselves. It is the first and highest duty of every person to learn from Scripture what is truth and then walk in truth and encourage others to follow Christ example. We should day by day study our Bible, weighing every thought and comparing scripture with scripture. We need to form our opinions for ourselves as we are to answer for ourselves before God. We should engage in our study of the Bible with a prayerful dependence upon God to learn His will for our life. We should never study God's Word without prayer !

We are living in the most solemn period of this world's history. The destiny of earth's multitudes is about to be decided. When the testing time shall come, those who have made God's Word the rule of life will be revealed. The false hearted Christians may not now be distinguished from the real, but time is just upon us when the difference will be apparent. Some who do not know what has been revealed about Christ coming, will fall for Satan's deceptions. Satan will deceive many when he has persons pretending to be Christ, preforming wonderful miracles of healing and professing to be the world's redeemer. How do we know this will take place? Matt 24:24—27—"There shall rise false prophets and show great sign's and wonders, in so much that, if it were possible, they shall deceive the very elect."

The great adversary 'Satan' now endeavors to gain by artifice what he has failed to secure by force. Persecution ceased, and in its stead will be substituted the dangerous allurements of temporal prosperity and world honor. Idolaters are led to receive a part of the Christian faith, while they rejected other essential truths. They professed to accept Jesus as the Son of God and to believe in His death and resurrection, but they have no conviction of sin and feel no need of repentance of a change of heart.

Under the clock of pretended Christianity, Satan is insinuating himself into the church, to corrupt faith and turn minds from the word of truth. there is two classes among those who profess to be followers of Christ. While one class studies the Savior's life and earnestly seek to correct their defects and conform to the Pattern, the other class shun the plain, practical truths which expose their errors. Christ did not turn Judas away. Judas yielded his mind to the control of the powers of Satan. Judas became angry when his faults were reproved, and he was led to commit the fearful crime of betraying his God. Do we today do the same when we are reproved of the error in our lives ? The day is coming when each person will make the choice to believe the Gospel of Truth or turn with the majority and accept what we like about the Gospel. Think about the majority who did not believe God and Noah about the coming flood. All those years to make a decision about what was the truth, what was to come, yet it was not comfortable to accept the truth for that day. Noah warned the people for 120 years what was coming. The truth is not always comfortable today as then, but the choice must be made by every person on earth.

It requires a desperate struggle for those who would be faithful to stand firm against the deceptions of Satan, and those who are disguised Christians in the church. The early Christians were indeed a peculiar people, and many paid with their lives. Though few in number, without wealth, position, or honorary titles, they were a terror to the evildoers wherever their character and doctrines were known.

Daniel 12:1—tells of a time coming-"a time of trouble coming, such as never was a nation, even to that same time; and at that time thy people shall be delivered, everyone that shall be found written in the book." Every case will have been decided for life or death. Christ has made the atonement for those who love's Him and has blotted out their sins. God's long-suffering will end for those who have rejected His mercy, despised His Love, and trampled upon His Law. The whole world will be involved in ruin more terrible than mankind can imagine. The special point of controversy throughout religious and secular authorities will combine to enforce the observance of the first day of the week as God's Sabbath. As Satan influenced Esau to march against his brother Jacob, to destroy him, so will Satan stir up the wicked to destroy God's people in the time of trouble coming upon the world. God's people have a promise in Rev 3:10—"I will keep thee from the hour of temptation, which shall come upon all the world." Those who have delayed their commitment to honor the Law of God, cannot obtain forgiveness at this time, because Christ has finished His work of judgment. Just like Judas, they will acknowledge their sin, though fear of punishment; but like Pharaoh of old, they would return to their defiance of heaven should the judgments of heaven be removed.

The trouble we see today around the earth, all the nations are in trouble. People are rioting and killing one another, full of hate for those leading the nation's and for those who acknowledge our Creator God of all that is good. People want the name of God removed from all things, and those who study the Scriptures know this is a sign of the end of time. How do we know this is the working's of Satan ? Rev 12:12—"Woe to the inhabitants of the earth and the sea! For the devil is come down to you, having great wrath, because he knows that he hath but a short time."

We know from Scripture that the end time is upon the world today. Scripture reveals that we will know when this is, Matt 24:6-14—"Wars and rumors of war,—nation against nation— famines and earthquakes in various places, people will hate one another; false prophets; lawlessness." Mark 13—"there will be earthquakes—famines, nation will rise against nation". Luke 21:5-38—"earthquakes—famines and pestilence." Do we see this in the world today ? Make a decision today to accept Christ and the Gospel of Truth and love. The day is coming when Christ will close His Book of Life and the great judgment day will be closed forever ! Those who have drifted along thinking of themselves, caring for themselves, will be placed by the Judge of the whole earth, with those who did evil. They receive the same condemnation.

There is only one way to heaven, we may not choose our own way. Christ say's "I am the way, no man cometh unto the Father, but by Me." Everyone who knows the Gospel truth for this time rest's the responsibility of making known to others, that we are nearing the time when Christ will come to take His people home to their eternal home, for eternity.

THE GOSPEL OF WHEN JESUS CHRIST COMES

Who will know when Jesus Christ comes? Rev 1:7—"Behold He cometh with clouds and 'every eye' shall see Him, and they also which pierced Him; and 'all' kindreds of the earth shall wail because of Him." Matt 24:27—"For as the lightning cometh out of the East, and shineth even to the west; so shall also the coming of the Son of Man be." V-30—"And then shall appear the sign of the Son of Man in heaven; and then shall all the tribes of the earth morn, and they shall see the Son of Man coming in the clouds of heaven with power and great glory." Matt 25:31—"When the Son of Man shall come in His glory, and all the Holy Angels with Him, then He shall sit upon the throne of His glory." 1 these 4:16-17—"For the Lord Himself shall descend from heaven with a shout, with the voice of the archangel, and with the trump of God, and the dead in Christ shall rise first; Then we which are alive and remain shall be caught up together with them in the clouds, to meet the Lord in the air; and so shall we ever be with the Lord." V-18—"Wherefore comfort one another with these words."

There is no possibility of Satan or any one of counterfeiting Christ coming! Christ coming will be universally known and witnessed by the whole world, every person on earth will witness Christ coming. Only those who have been diligent students of Scripture and love the truth of the Gospel will be shielded from the powerful delusion that takes the world captive, as Satan will try to deceive the world. Matt 24:27—"For as the lighting comes from the East and flashes to the west, so also will the coming of the Lord be." V-31—"and He will send His angels with a great sound of a trumpet, and they will gather together His elect from the four winds, from one end of the heavens to the other."

People today may not understand why Christ will gather together, dead and living, to take to heaven to live with Him. Do you really think that those who rejected Christ while Jesus walked this earth, could accept the fact they were wrong about the Mission of Jesus now ? Those who rejected then, claiming He saved others, but not Himself, rejected Jesus Christ because then, they could not except the fact they were wrong about the mission of Christ. People today are just as the people then, they cannot accept the fact they and the majority of the world can be wrong about how and when Christians should worship the God of Love. Many do not accept the Sabbath of the Lord that He created on the seventh day of Creation Week. People today are like the people when Christ walked this earth, They would rather have a 'Barabbas', a subtitled christ and religion as to acknowledge the Truth of God. Not all people have the knowledge of Scripture but they trust in the Lord for what they know. Our Lord knows that some don't have access to the Gospel and they will be judged by what they know.

Satan will try to impersonate Christ coming and will appear in different parts on the earth and people that don't know what the Gospel says will go to see. How do we know this? Scripture tells that this will happen.

Suppose that today Christ should appear in the clouds of heaven, who would be ready to meet Him ? Suppose we should be translated into the kingdom of heaven just as we are. Would we be prepared to unite with the saints of God, to live in harmony with the royal family, the children of the heavenly King ? Are we seeking to help others around us, that are not keeping the Law of God which is the Law of all the universe ? Are we getting ready to meet the King of the universe ? How many of us is ready to receive the crown of Life? Position does not make the person ready. It was Christ who formed us in the womb and makes us worthy of receiving the crown of life, that fadeth not away.

Mark 13:6—"Many will come in My name and deceive many." Luke 17:23-24—"Some will say look here ! Look there ! Do not go after them. For as the lighting flashes out of one part of heaven, so also the Son of Man will be in His day."

Satan cannot counterfeit the coming of Christ, for every eye on earth will see Christ come in the clouds, not just here or somewhere !

THE GOSPEL OF THE THOUSAND YEARS IN HEAVEN, THEN WHAT IS TO COME?

For a thousand years, the saints will search the books of heaven to understand why some people, maybe loved ones chose not to accept the Gospel of God and are not there. God is Love, and he will not force people against their will—choice.—1 Corinthians 6:2-3.

The people who made the choice to Honor our Creator God and His Law will judge those who are not saved. Every person has to make their choice for themselves. God will not make our choice for us. Love does not mandate what others should do.

At the end of the thousand years of God's people being in heaven with Christ with all the Holy angels and the people who love Jesus Christ and loves His Law, then what? This is when the second resurrection will take place. Christ bids the wicked dead to arise, to receive their choice of not to be with Christ or to honor His Law of Love. They come forth, a mighty host, numberless as the sands of the sea. What a contrast to those who were raised at the first resurrection ! The righteous were clothed with immortal youth and beauty. The wicked bear the traces of disease and death. With one voice the wicked proclaim; "Blessed is He that cometh in the name of the Lord !" The force of "truth" urges the words from unwilling lips. All see that their exclusion from heaven is just. By their lives, they have declared, "We will not have this man

'Jesus' to reign over us." Satan and all those with him see that their exclusion from heaven is just. Satan looks upon his kingdom, the fruit of his toil, he sees only failure and ruin.

In the first resurrection, only those who chose to accept and live by the Gospel are raised from the graves and taken to heaven with those who are alive, to be with Jesus Christ and those who accepted the Gospel.

"At the close of the thousand years, Christ bids the wicked dead to rise, to receive their fate". Rev 20:5—"But the rest of the dead lived not until the thousand years were finished. This is the first resurrection of those who were not taken to heaven at Christ coming. Rev 20:6—"blessed and Holy is he that hath part in the first resurrection; on such the second death hath no power, but they shall be priests of God and of Christ, and shall reign with Him a thousand years." V-7—"And when the thousand years are expired, Satan shall be loosed out of his prison." V-8—"And Satan shall go out to deceive the nations which are in the four corners of the earth, Gog and Magog to gather them together to battle; the number of them is as the sands of the sea." All these people are the people who refused to believe the Gospel and chose to believe as those before the Flood.

Why does Satan and his angels seek to gather these people that are raised from the dead at the end of the thousand years ? The people who have honored and loved Christ and His Law of Love, and the Gospel of Truth and Love, that God gave to mankind to live by, are safe with Christ in heaven. Satan does not accept the Law of God and wants and believes that he and those who like him, who don't honor the Law of Love, can now over throw the Kingdom of God. The people who have chosen to love the Gospel of Truth and Love, are safe inside the Holy City which Christ will bring back to this earth when He destroys sin and those who did not want to live by The Gospel. Oh that people could realize that

Christ wants to save them if they would only live according to His Gospel of Love, which is simple. Heaven could not be a peaceful place if everyone wanted to live by their own gospel. Make plans today to be part of God's family while on this earth today and look forward to Christ coming to take us home to heaven.

At the close of the thousand years, the wicked are raised from the dead and appear before God for the execution of the judgment written. The righteous were clothed with immortal youth and beauty when they came from the grave. The wicked bear the traces of disease and death. In that vast throng of people that will be raised at the end of the thousand years will be all the multitude of people who lived before the flood, men of lofty stature and giant intellect, kings and generals who conquered nations, men who never lost a battle. The only battle the wicked have lost is the battle of Good and Evil. Satan and his subjects have no power to turn from the picture of their own work in life now. Each will recall how they turned away from the Gospel of Truth and will seek to hide from the Divine Majesty. It is now evident to 'all' that the wages of sin is death, and not noble independence and eternal life, but slavery, ruin, and death. All will see that their exclusion from heaven is just. By their lives they have declared; "We will not have this Man 'Jesus' to reign over us." For thousands of years, the wicked will see that Satan has conspired to palm off falsehood for Truth. The results of rebellion and the results of setting aside the Law of Love, The history of sin will stand to all eternity as a witness that with the existence of God's Law is bound up in happiness of the beings God has created.

In a voice that reaches the assembled multitudes of the righteous and the wicked, Christ declared; "Behold the purchase of My blood! For these I suffered, for these I died, that they might dwell in My presence through-out eternal ages." Where will you be when you hear this voice of Christ? Hopefully you will be with all those who love God, His Son who died for you, and those who love God's Law of Love !

At the end of the thousand years, the Gospel says Ezekiel 28:6-8 & 16-19—"I will bring thee to ashes upon the earth in sight of all them that behold thee—Thou shalt be a terror, and never shalt thou be any more." Mal 4:1—"for a day is coming, burning like an oven. All the proud, yes, all who do wickedly will be stubble. And the day which is coming shall burn them up, says the Lord of hosts, That will leave them neither root nor branch." No eternal burning hell will be kept before the ransomed, the fearful consequences of sin. Only one reminder remains—the Marks of Christ crucifixion, His hands and feet, are the only traces of the cruel work that sin has wrought.

THE GOSPEL ABOUT THE DAY EVIL DIES; THEN WHAT?

The question many ask is "Why did God allow sin to be committed ? The government of God is based upon a Love relationship and it must have free choice fully operative. Even Satan must be allowed his freedom to reveal his true nature. So at the final gathering of the lost for slaughter, Satan must be unmasked. His whole philosophy has been "If I have to die and miss out on heaven, I'm going to take as many as possible with me." When the universe witnesses his final gathering of the lost for slaughter, they will have a further testimony that is consistent with the agony of Calvary to verify the nature of Satan's rebellion in contrast to God's nature of Love.

At the second coming of Christ the wicked are blotted from the face of the earth, consumed with the Spirit of His mouth and destroyed by the brightness of His glory. Why? Isa 24:1,3,5-6—"Behold the Lord makes the earth empty, and makes it waste."—"The land shall be entirely emptied and utterly plundered, for the Lord has spoken this word."—"the earth is also defiled under its inhabitants, Because they have transgressed the Laws, changed the Ordinance. Broken the everlasting covenant."— "Therefore the inhabitants of the earth are burned up. And a few men are left."

Rev 20:1-3—"An angel coming down from heaven, having the key to the bottomless pit and a great chain in his hand. He lays hold of the dragon "Satan" the serpent of old, who is the Devil and Satan, and bound him for a thousand years; —and shut him up, and set a seal on him, so that he should deceive the nations no more till the thousand years were finished. But after these things he must be released for a little while."

During the thousand years between the first and second resurrection, the judgment of the wicked takes place in heaven by the righteous. ! Cor 6:2-3—"Do you not know that the saints will judge the world?" V-3—"Do you not know that the 'Saints' shall judge the angels?" These angels are the angels who sided with Lucifer in heaven and were put out of heaven.

Christ takes only those home to heaven who love and obey His Gospel. What would heaven be like if those who choose to honor and love as they choose were to be allowed to live with those who love the Law of the universe ? Christ is choosing now those who choose to honor and Love His Law of the Universe. Christ is not judging the wicked, He leaves that to the people that love Christ and live according to His Gospel.

For six thousand years, Satan's work of rebellion has made the earth tremble, a prison house for those who love the Lord. The earth has received God's people and Satan would hold them forever in the graves if he could. Christ broke Satan's bonds when Jesus came to this earth and died for the sins of people, but only those that choose to live as Christ has asked in His Holy Word, will He accept to take home to heaven.

The history of sin will stand through all eternity as a witness, that with the existence of God's Law is bound up the happiness of all the beings God has created. For six thousand years Satan has wrought his will, filling the earth with woe and causing grief through out God's universe. God's people will forever be delivered from Satan's presence and temptations.

Only one reminder alone remains; our Savior will ever bear the marks of His crucifixion. Upon His wounded head, upon His hands and feet, are the only traces of the cruel work of sin ! The tokens of His humiliation are His highest honor; through eternal ages.

This earth, originally given to man as his kingdom, was betrayed by him into the hands of Satan, and has been held by the mighty foe, will be brought back by the great plan of redemption. 1 Corinthians 2:9—"Eye hath not seen, nor ear heard, neither have entered into the heart of man, the things which God hath prepared for them that love Him." Isa 45:18—"God Himself formed the earth and made it; He hath established it; He created it not in vain, He formed it to be inhabited. I am the Lord, and there is none else."

What will the people that are redeemed do when our Lord clears this earth from sin? Isa 32:18—"My people shall dwell in a peaceable habitation, and in sure dwellings; and in a great resting place." Isa 60:18—"Violence shall be no more heard in the land, wasting nor destruction within thy borders." Isa 66:21—"And they shall build houses, and inhabit; and they shall plant vineyards, and eat the fruit of them." V-22—"They shall not build and another inhabit; They shall not plant, and another eat, for as the days of a tree are the days of My people, and mine elect shall long enjoy the work of their hands." Isa 66:23—"And it shall come to pass that from one new moon to another, and from one Sabbath to another, shall all flesh come to worship before Me, saith the Lord.

There will be a New Jerusalem, that will glorify the new earth, there will be no night there—Rev 21:23-25. The redeemed shall know, even as also they are known. The redeemed will have communion with Holy beings, and harmonious social life with the blessed angels and the faithful ones of all ages.

There will be no cruel, deceiving foe to tempt forgetfulness of God. All the treasures of the universe will be open to the study of God's redeemed. As knowledge is progressive, so will love, reverence, and happiness increase. The more people learn of God, the greater will be their admiration of His character.

From the minutest atom to the greatest world, all things declare, "God is Love." Everything that God has created has 'love' built in it. How you and I deal with love "This God given Gift", will determine our future destination.

We only need to remember how Noah preached for 120 years, and how many believed the Gospel then that the world was going to be destroyed by a flood ! Do you believe the world today is receiving the Gospel any better ?

Remember, God loves you. He came and died to cover your sins and everyone's sins with His blood. What will you say when you see Christ coming in the clouds of heaven ? Will it be—"Lo this is my God or will you cry for the rocks and hills to fall on you to hide you from the One who loves you and died for you ?

Rom 1:16—"For I am not ashamed of the Gospel of Christ, for it is the power of God unto salvation for everyone who believes; for the Jew first and also for the Greek." Isa 49:26—"all flesh will know that I am the Lord, Saviour, and Redeemer." No one will be able to say they didn't know, for Scripture says all will know but the decision is left to each person. Please decide today, for we are not promised tomorrow !

WHAT DOES THE GOSPEL SAY ABOUT THE LORD'S DAY?

Many people today say they worship on the Lord's day. You have also heard some say that it doesn't make any difference what day a person keeps for a Sabbath day, just so its one of the seven. But the Bible says differently. In the New Testament, the book of Revelation tells us that there is a day that is the Lord's Day. There is one day that belongs to God—the Lord's Day. In Revelation 1:19—John said "I was in the Spirit on the Lord's day." There is a day that belongs to God —a day that is the Lord's, that is special and belongs to our Creator.

Now John doesn't say what day of the week is the Lord's day in this verse. He doesn't say weather it is Sabbath or the first day of the week. But we find that Jesus answers our question in Matthew 12:8. Jesus Himself speaks and tells us which is the Lord's day. Here He says, "For the Son of Man is Lord of the Sabbath day." Then according to the testimony of Jesus, it is the Sabbath day that is His Holy Day, the Lord's day. In Mark 2:27-28—we read the same thing again—that Jesus is "Lord also of the Sabbath." Then the Sabbath must be the Lord's Day.

But we say, "But we still haven't learned for certain which day of the week is the Sabbath day. God wants us to recognize that one day is His. Jesus says it is the Sabbath, but is the Sabbath the seventh day of the week, or could it be first day of the week? We read the answer to that also in the New Testament. In Hebrews 4:4—"For He spoke of a certain place of the seventh day on this wise, and God did rest the seventh day on this wise, And God did rest the seventh day from all His works." Twice in the same same verse in the New Testament it tells us that the seventh day is God's rest day, His Sabbath. In Mark 2:27—28 we read the same thing again—that Jesus is "Lord also of the Sabbath." Then the Sabbath is the Lord's Day.

We read in Exodus 20:8-11 "The seventh day is the Sabbath of the Lord thy God." It is not the Jews sabbath or a Sabbath for any special dispensation. It is the Sabbath of the Lord, it is the Lord's day. When you stop to think about it, the Bible makes it so simple that we wonder how anyone could be confused. If we just follow the words of Jesus, it is so plain that it is impossible to misunderstand.

Can we be certain that the seventh day that we honor today, 'Saturday' is the same as the seventh day of Jesus time? Has the calendar been changed and has time been lost? Well, the calendar has been changed in history, but time has never been lost. Russia changed it's calendar in 1914, the last among modern nations to do so. They lost several days as far as the calendar was concerned, but the weekly cycle was never changed—Wednesday followed Tuesday, for instance. Each time the calendar has been changed, the sequence of days in the week has remained the same. We can know that our weekly cycle is the same as that of Abraham's time.

Archaeologists have dug up clay tablets and monuments dating back to Abraham's time that tell about eclipses of the sun and moon and give the day of the week on which they happened. And all this agrees that no time has been lost. So if Jesus our Saviour, knew which day He was Lord of, then I can know which day is the Sabbath and honor the Sabbath of our Lord.

The Bible tells us also how the days of the week are lined up. Luke 23 and 24, we are told which day Jesus died and was buried, which day He rested in the tomb, and which day He was resurrected. All today are familiar with these days of the week.

Which day was Jesus crucified on ? Friday. On which day was Jesus resurrected ? On Sunday. Now then, if this is true, let us look at these three text of Scripture. Luke 23:52-56, says—"This man 'Joseph of Arimathea' went to Pilate and asked for the body of Jesus. Then he took Jesus down from the cross and wrapped Him in a linen shroud, and laid Him in a rock-hewed tomb, where no one had ever been laid. It was the day of Preparation, which is the day before the Sabbath. On the Sabbath Day the followers of Jesus rested according to the commandment. Notice this, because it makes it very clear that the Sabbath 'according to the commandment' was the day following the crucifixion and burial of Jesus. Jesus rested in death on the Sabbath day according to the commandment. The Apostles rested on the Sabbath and we read in the next chapter that "On the first day of the week, early dawn, they went to the tomb, taking the spices which they had prepared. They found the stone rolled away from the tomb, but when they went in, they did not find the body of Jesus—Luke 24:1-3.

It is a mystery how people when asked why they keep Sunday, the first day of the week for the Sabbath which Jesus kept, even while in the 'tomb'. Some say they keep the first day of the week in honor of Christ resurrection day. But some will often tell you that time has been lost and we don't know for sure what day is the Sabbath. It is a mystery how people can be so sure which day is the first day of the week to keep in honor of His resurrection, but then can never tell which day is the seventh day ! Jesus gave us the Sabbath keeping example while He was on earth. The Bible did predict in the prophecies of Daniel and Paul, that there would come a change, and there would be an effort to change the 'time' element in God's Law. There is only one of the ten commandments that has to do with time and that is the Sabbath. The Bible did predict that a change would come. It took over three hundred years for the complete change to come about in Rome. In other areas the Sabbath was kept for more than a thousand years after Christ returned to heaven. This apostasy first started in Rome and from there it branched out over Christendom along with many other apostasies as well.

Dr E. T. Hiscox, the great Baptist scholar who wrote the Baptist Manual, asked, where can the record of such a transaction as changing God's Sabbath from the seventh day to the first day be found? "Not in the new Testament—absolutely not." There is no Scriptural evidence of the Sabbath institution from the seventh to the first day of the week. But what a pity that it comes branded with the mark of paganism and christened with the name of the sun-god. No where in the Bible is it laid down that worship should be done on Sunday. It is a matter of our loyalty and our allegiance to God or to man. On one hand there is Christ and His day. On the other, the day of man's tradition. I think of Joshua in Scripture when he drew a line and said, "Who is on the Lord's side?" Then he stepped over that line and challenged the children of Israel to step over with him. He said "As for me and my house, we will serve the Lord"—Joshua 24:15. There would never have been the theory of evolution if the Sabbath had been faithfully kept.

The Bible says that —"from one new moon to another, and from one Sabbath to another, all flesh will come to worship before Me saith the Lord"—Isa 66:23. The sabbath will be the eternal memorial of God's creative power. The Sabbath gives the reason why God is God. Other gods could give nine of the ten commandments, but there is only one God who can say, "Remember the Sabbath Day to keep it Holy, for in six days the Lord made the Heavens and the Earth." Is it any wonder God gave the Sabbath as an emblem of our loyalty and love for Him ?

The colors of red, white and blue are just colors, but when these colors are put on cloth and sewed into our U S A flag, do they mean something to you? As American citizens, we have made it something special. God took an ordinary day, and He sanctified and hallowed it and made it a Sabbath, a symbol of His creative power. Can you and I trample on that symbol of His Love for us, of His power in creating us ? Is it any wonder that God pleads with us in Isaiah 58:13-14, "If you turn away your foot from the Sabbath, from doing your pleasure on My Holy day. And call the Sabbath a delight, The Holy day of the Lord honorable, And shall honor Him, not doing your ways, nor finding your own pleasure, nor speaking your own words, Then you shall delight yourself in the Lord; And I will cause you to ride on the high hills of the earth, And feed you with the heritage of Jacob your father. The mouth of the Lord has spoken." God begs us to keep the sabbath and if we will we shall receive a blessing.

Friend, what will you judge 'truth' by, a Galloup poll or by popularity contest ? Jesus said Broad is the way that leads -"where' to destruction, and many their be that go in there at; because strait is the gate and narrow is the way which leadeth unto life and few their be that find it,—Matt 7:13-14. We must judge 'truth' by a thus saith the Lord.' The pagans of all ages have kept Sunday, worshiping the sun of that day. There are Popes and ministers of many churches who teach that it makes no difference about keeping God's commandments. There are many sincere Christians who have have followed these leaders, never questioning, and God understands. We think of those who in the past that followed God's commandments, Enoch, Noah, David, Isaiah, Paul, Peter, James, John and many others. As we weigh the eternal consequences of our decision, Jesus lifts His nail scarred hands, and says, "If you love Me keep My commandments." Friend, where will stand when Christ comes ?

Many today say they worship on the Lord's day. What does the Scripture's say about the Lord's Day ? Isa 13:6—"Wail;, for the day of the Lord is at hand ! It will come as destruction from the almighty" V-9—"Behold, the day of the Lord comes, Cruel, with both wrath and fierce anger, to lay the land desolate; And He will destroy the sinners from it." V-10—For the stars of heaven and their constellations will not give their light; the sun will be darkened in it's going forth. And the moon will not cause its light to shine." V-11—"I will punish the world for its evil, And the wicked for their iniquity; I will halt the arrogance of the proud, and will lay low the haughtiness of the terrible." V-13—"I will shake the heavens and the earth will move out of her place." Amos 5:18-19—"Woe to you who desire the day of the Lord ! For what good is the day of the Lord to you ? Obadiah 15—"The day of the Lord is near—as you have done, so it will be done to you; Your reprisal shall return upon your own head. Zeph 1:2-3—"I will consume both man and beast; birds of the heavens, fish of the sea, and the stumbling blocks along with the wicked. I will cut off man from the face of the land." V-14—18—"The great day of the Lord is near, the mighty men will cry out, That day is a day of wrath, A day of trouble and distress, A day of devastation and desolation. A day of darkness and gloominess, A day of clouds and darkness—I will bring distress upon men, and they will walk like blind men, because they have sinned against the Lord. —"Neither will their silver nor their gold, shall be able to deliver them in the day of the Lord's wrath; —He will make a speedy riddance of all those who dwell in the land." Zech 14:12—"Their flesh shall dissolve while they stand on their feet." 1 Thess 5:2—"For you yourselves know perfectly well, that the day of the Lord so comes as a thief in the night."

TWO GROUPS; POWERS AT THE END OF THIS WORLD IN SCRIPTURE

There will be two powers or groups of Christians that will claim to be the true followers of Scripture and Christ. Who and how do we know which to belong to and why should we belong to either ?

The largest group of Christians are of the Roman Catholic Universal Church. The smaller group is made up of many different faiths. Some claim Sunday, the first day of the week as God's Holy Day for worship and the smaller group worships on the seventh day of the Scripture's Sabbath.

Revelation 13—speaks of those two groups. One is God's true church preaching the Gospel to all the world, "To every nation, kindred, tongue and people." the other is the apostate, counterfeit church having power over all kindreds and nations and tongues, which is a blaspheming power that is counterfeiting the Gospel of God in Scripture. This power claims the names of God for its leaders, "The Holy Father". Rev 13 says all those who dwell on the earth will worship this beast power whose names are not written in the book of Life of the Lamb slain from the foundation of the world.

Friend, all the world is wondering after this beast power, forty-seven nations are officially represented there in Rome. We can know that we are not part of this group that claim to be the true and faithful church. How do we know—1 John 2:3,5—"By this we know we are His if we keep His commandments." So it has always been. Scripture says in Isaiah—"Bind up the testimony, seal the Law among My disciples"-Ezekiel 20:12, 20—"Moreover also, I gave them My Sabbaths that they might be a sign between Me and them, that they may know that I am the Lord who sanctifies them." God knew that while it would be popular to keep nine of the ten commandments in our day, there would be one, the Sabbath, which would become the deciding factor as to whether we would keep all His commandments or not.

It is because this commandment is so universally disregarded that God knew ahead of time that the keeping of the Sabbath would make a difference. The Sabbath command is the only one of the ten which includes; His name "God" His title "Creator", His realm "Heaven and earth". Now as we learn of the great counterfeit mark of the beast power, we shall see still another reason why God chose and foreknew the Sabbath as His sign and seal.

This Roman church power stands firmly on the basis that; "Tradition", not Scripture is the rock on which the church is built. Daniel predicted in Daniel 7:25—"that there would be one to think to change times and laws." The early church councils took certain actions changing to Sunday as the Sabbath. There is no text in the Bible that gives authority, actions changing to Sunday as the Sabbath. There is no text in the Bible that gives authority for this change. Protestants broke away from the Catholic Church in the 15th and 16th centuries but thy did not go back to the Bible Sabbath; they are still following the Roman Church in the observance of Sunday as the Sabbath.

The Roman Church leaders say that if the churches followed the Bible only, they would observe the Lord's Day on Saturday, the Sabbath of the Lord, for the Bible can be searched from Genesis to the end of Revelation, and find no command, that in Christian practice, the day of rest and worship should be observed on Sunday.

God has His Mark which is the memorial of His creator-ship, His deity—the seventh-day Sabbath. Then the great counterfeit plan of salvation which substitutes the Holy system of worship to the first day is a counterfeit. People who don't know how and when man brought this counterfeit sabbath are not held accountable. James 4:17; Acts 17:30; Rom 2:12,16. It is a sin at any time to disobey God's Law when we know what we should do and then follow the way of the world because it is easier !

Every person will face a great test when we decide if we will follow God or man. 2 Thessalonians 2:9-12—"If they receive not the love of the Truth that they might be saved—but have pleasure in unrighteousness, God will send strong delusion and they will believe a lie, that they all might be damned."

> Once to every man and nation,
> Comes the moment to decide,
> In the strife twixt truth or falsehood
> For the good or evil side.

We either love the Truth and follow it, or we begin to excuse ourselves for disregarding it. If we begin to make excuses, we will believe them before very long. The day we keep reveals our allegiance and loyalty to our Lord. Rom 6:16—"Know ye not that to whom ye yield yourselves servants to obey, His servants ye are whom ye obey" !

Most of the world bows down to worship the power which presumed to change God's Law and counterfeit Gods work. Most of the world today obeys the power of the one that is king in their life. They are servants to him. Those who are seeking to be faithful to God may be denied many of the privileges of the world; but there is no power that can close the door of communication between God and our souls. Every day we have the privilege of connecting ourselves with Christ, and we may draw daily supplies of Grace. Neither men nor Satan can close the door which Christ has opened for us. Rev 3:8—"Behold, I have set before thee an open door, and no man can shut it."

Sense Cain and Able, there has been conflict between those who choose to follow Christ and those who want to do as they choose. Christ and those who follow Christ, has and will have conflict in this world, because Satan has claimed this world as his. He even offered this world to Jesus Christ if Jesus would bow down and worship him—Matt 4:8-10. How did the world treat and accept the Gospel of Jesus Christ when He walked among people on this earth ? Are Christians accepted any more today ? Those in power while Jesus was on earth put Christ on a cross and mocked Him as King of the Jews. Are people mocked today when they follow the Gospel ? Some today are ridiculed because they have chosen to follow the Gospel. But those who do this do not know the end of the story. One day, the heavens will be rolled back and Jesus will come in the clouds of glory. While those who have rejected will be crying for the rocks and mountains to fall on them and hide them from His Majesty, those who have received and kept His commandments, will look up and say, "Lo, this is our God, we have waited for Him and He will save us." They will lift their voices with the angels to sing; All hail the power of Jesus name. Have you made your choice?

WHAT DOES SCRIPTURE
SAY ABOUT ANGELS?

The Scriptures not only teach the existence of angels, but both good and evil, but present unquestionable proof that these are not disembodied spirits of dead men. Angels are in nature superior to man, for the Psalmist says that man was made —"a little lower than the angels."-Ps 8:5.

Daniel had a vision of the angels in heaven Daniel 7:10—"Thousand thousands ministered unto Him, and ten thousand times ten thousand stood before Him; the judgment was set and the books were opened." In Hebrews 12:22—"an innumerable company of angels," Angels are sent on missions of mercy to the children of God. We have recorded in Scripture some of the times God sent His angels to mankind. To Abraham with promises of blessings and to Lot who lived in Sodom just before God destroyed the city of wicked people. To Elijah just before he was about to perish from weariness and hunger in the desert. To Daniel with divine wisdom about the writings on the wall, and protection while in the lion's den. To Peter who was doomed to death in Herod's dungeon. A Guardian angel is appointed to every follower of Christ. How do we know this ? Ps 34:7—"The angel of the Lord encamps round about them that fear Him, and delivers them."

Christian's who follow Christ are ever safe under His watch care. Angels that excel in strength are sent from heaven to protect them. the wicked one cannot break through the guard which God has stationed about His people.

SIGNS OF THE END OF TIME FOR THIS WORLD

The whole world is in agitation. The Spirit of God is being withdrawing from this earth, and calamity follows calamity by sea and by land. There are tempests, earthquakes, fires, floods, murders of every grade, fires break out unexpectedly and no human effort will be able to quench them. Hatred for one another in high places of Government, confusion, collision and death without a moments warning will occur on the great lines of travel.

The warning that Christ is coming soon has become to many a familiar tale. The same spirit existed as in the days of Noah. the seed of unbelief and evil is not readily rooted up.

The end of the world, is about to come to the end, probation is closing, seek God while He may be found. Do not wait for a convent time. Who knows if we might be here tomorrow ? Jesus gave His life for you and me, but Jesus left the choice to each person, for that is the way Love is manifested to His creations !

Rev 1:3—"Blessed is he that reads, and they that hear the words of this prophecy, and keep those things which are written there in, for the time is at hand." Rev 22:19—and If any man shall take away from the words of the book of this prophecy, God shall take away his part from the book of life, from the Holy City, and from the things which are written in this book."

IT IS FINISHED!

Two times Christ has or will say "IT IS FINISHED" The first time while He was on earth, while He was on the Cross dying for our sins. The next time will be when Christ finishes His Judgment in heaven of those who love Him. Rev 22:11—"He that is unjust, let him be unjust still; and he that is filthy, let him be filthy still; and he who is righteous, let him be righteous still; and he that is holy, let him be holy still." All judgment will be over "finished" when Jesus Christ comes in the clouds to redeem those who love His Gospel. Christ judgment will be finished, and Christ will come to redeem those who love their Creator and their fellow man and abide by His Law of Love and have faith in the Words of God. Rev 12:2—"And many of those who sleep in the dust of the earth shall awake. Some to everlasting life, Some to shame and everlasting contempt." Those that are saved have loved Christ much because they have been forgiven much. Love will determine our future. What do you and I love more? The love of our Creator or the things of this world, which will perish with those who have refused the Gospel of Truth and Love? Never will it be forgotten that He whose power created and upholds the worlds, came to this earth and bore the guilt and shame of sin, that His creation might be restored. Christ bore our sins on His cross that we might be restored and have a home with our Creator God. The Kingdom of God does not have an end, His Kingdom is eternal !

Let no one feel that he or she is stepping down in becoming a child of God. It was the only begotten Son of God who stepped down. Jesus hung upon Calvary's cross, dying in our behalf, that we might have eternal life. It seems a small thing that Jesus should endure all this, that we might be called the sons of God ? Does it seem a small thing to you to become members of the Royal family, children of the heavenly King, partakers of an immortal inheritance? We are not our own, we are bought with a price. Each one of us has to make a choice today. We have no promise of tomorrow!

Rev 20, tells of those who have accepted the Gospel of Truth in "God's Word"-"Bible", and also of those who choose not to believe the Gospel of Truth. God, Himself will dwell with those who love and obey His Gospel, His Law of Love, His commandments. There will be no more death, neither sorrow, or crying, neither shall their be any more pain; for former things are passed away. God will give unto him that is athirst of the fountain of the water of life freely. I will be his God, and he shall be My son. Rev 20, also tells what is to happen to those who have refused to believe the Gospel of Truth and Love ! "But the fearful, and unbelieving and the abominable, and murderers, and whore mongers, and sorcerers, and idolaters, and all liars, shall have their part in the lake which burns with fire and brimstone, which is the second death." No one on earth needs to be forgotten or refuse the Gospel of Truth. Make a discision now and never turn back to what the world believes. God's Truth is everlasting, eternal. what did Jesus tell the rich young ruler about how to inherit eternal life? Luke 18:18-23—"You know the commandments." What did the rich young ruler say and do ? He went away very sorrowful, for he was very rich. What do people do or say today about their salvation and why can't people honor and obey God's simple Ten rule's of commandments ? All the commandments of God are about "Love". Romans 15:4—"For whatever things were written before were written for our learning, that we through the patience and comfort of the Scriptures might have hope." Other text that help us to know what sin is that we can overcome sin— Rom 3:20,31— James 4:17—Ezekiel 18:20—1 Peter 3:18—1 Cor 15:20-21— James 1:13-15—1 Cor 10:13—John 10:27-30. What promise's we are given from our Creator to help us understand a plan for our every-day life and for a life and home with our Creator God.

The morning and the night are both at the same time for all people on earth. The opening of the endless day to the righteous, and the eternal night to the wicked who refuse the Gospel and Love of God.

Dear Friend, I want to leave it the way God says it in His book, don't you? That's much better than to think that God will receive some sadistic pleasure throughout the ceaseless ages of eternity by tormenting those who refused to believe the Gospel. The Bible calls it Isa 28:21—"His strange act of destroying the wicked.

WHAT DOES THE GOSPEL SAY, AFTER SIN IS DESTROYED?

REV 21:1,4—"Now I saw a new heaven and a new earth, for the first heaven and the first earth had passed away. Also there was no more sea." "God shall wipe away all tears from their eyes, and there shall be no more death, neither sorrow, nor crying, neither shall there be any more pain, for the former things are pasted away." Ps 37:29—"The righteous shall inherit the land, and dwell therein forever." Heb 11:16—"Therefore, God is not ashamed to be called their God, for He has prepared a city for them."

There will be no cruel, deceiving foe to tempt the forgetfulness of God. The great controversy is ended. Sin and sinners are no more. From Him who created all, flow life and light and gladness throughout all of God's creations. Isa 65:17—"For behold, I create new heavens and a new earth, and the former shall not be remembered or come to mind." V-19—"The voice of weeping shall no longer be heard, nor the voice of crying." V-21—"They shall build houses and inhabit them, they shall plant vineyards and eat their fruit." V-25—"the wolf and the lamb shall feed together, and the lion shall eat straw like the ox. And the dust shall be the serpent's food. They shall not hurt nor destroy in all My Holy mountain.

Isa 66:22—"For as the new heavens and the new earth which I will make remain before Me, says the Lord. So shall your descendants and your name remain. And it shall come to pass that from one new moon to another, and from one Sabbath to another 'all flesh' shall come to worship before Me, says the Lord."

Is it possible that mankind was created because God wanted the angels to know and to see for themselves why the Lord could not have rebellion and sin to exist in heaven? God's Kingdom is a Kingdom of Love and selfish desires leads to sin, which cannot exist in the kingdom of God. Rev 21:4—gives us knowledge of what heaven will be like for those who love our Lord. V—27— "But there shall by no means enter into it anything that defiles, or causes an abomination, or a lie; but only those who are written in the Lamb's book of life." Do you want your name written there? Love for Jesus Christ our Lord and Savior and our fellow man and obedience to God's law prove our Love that God's Grace reveals that we desire to be with our Creator God.

In the work of redemption there is no compulsion. No external force is employed. Man is left to choose whom he will serve, We have no power to free ourselves from Satan's control. But when we desire to be set free from sin; the powers of the soul are imbued with divine energy of the Holy Spirit, and they obey the dictates of the will in fulfilling the will of God. "The truth shall make you free." "Christ is the Truth." No matter who you are or what you may have done, if you are willing, God will accept you and you can change your life, and know God will help you to know His saving Grace. We only need to read the Scripture how Jesus loved Mary the prostitute and she changed her life from slavery to following Christ, who wants to save every person He created, but leaves to us the choice. Mary was the first to see Jesus from the tomb and proclaim our risen Savior. The Gospel of the kingdom shall be preached in all the world for a witness unto all nations; and then shall Christ come. God has provided for every person an opportunity to know that which will make them wise unto salvation.

Everything in this world is in agitation. The spirit of God is withdrawing from the earth, and calamity follows calamity by sea and by land. There are tempests, earthquakes, fires, floods, murders of every grade. Rapidly are men ranging themselves under the banner they have chosen. have you made your choice ? I pray you will make your choice to accept the Gospel from the Holy Bible that our Lord has preserved and provided before it's to late. God help us all to accept all the Truth from His Word. Many will be lost while hoping and desiring to be Christians, but they make no earnest effort, therefore they will be weighed in the balances and found wanting. It is no easy matter to gain the priceless treasure of eternal life. No one can do this and drift with the world. The same spirit of selfishness, of conformity to the practices of the world, exists in our day as in Noah's day. All are by their own choice deciding their destiny, and God is overruling all for the accomplishment of His purposes. if professed Christians love Jesus more than the world, they will love to speak of Him, their best friend, in whom their highest affections are centered. Beware, Satan will present the path of holiness as difficult while the paths of worldly pleasure are strewed with flowers. But remember the pleasures of earth will have an end. No matter who you are or what your life has been, you can be saved only in God's way.

I am praying that this book has helped you understand the Gospel and direct your life, for today and for eternity. Romans 1:16—"For I am not ashamed of the Gospel of Christ; for it is the power of God unto salvation to every one that believes." James 1:22—"But be ye doers of the Word, not hearers only, deceiving your selves."

The more you search the Holy Scriptures with a humble heart, the greater will be your interest. Pray for wisdom and understanding as you read the Holy Writings. The last verse in the Scriptures [Revelation 22:20-21—"He who testifies to these things says, 'Surely I am coming quickly.' amen. Even so, come Lord Jesus ! The grace of our Lord Jesus Christ be with you all. Amen."

May this be your and my prayer—"God, I don't care what people think of me today, but I car about what they think of Your Son because of me today !" God help each one to prepare today to look up and say when we see our Lord in the air —"Lo, this is my God ! AMEN.

Printed in the United States
By Bookmasters